D0927754

FREE

Free Study Tips DVD

In addition to the tips and content in this guide, we have created a FREE DVD with helpful study tips to further assist your exam preparation. **This FREE Study Tips DVD provides you with top-notch tips to conquer your exam and reach your goals.**

Our simple request in exchange for the strategy-packed DVD packed is that you email us your feedback about our study guide. We would love to hear what you thought about the guide, and we welcome any and all feedback—positive, negative, or neutral. It is our #1 goal to provide you with top quality products and customer service.

To receive your **FREE Study Tips DVD**, email freedvd@apexprep.com. Please put "FREE DVD" in the subject line and put the following in the email:

    a. The name of the study guide you purchased.

    b. Your rating of the study guide on a scale of 1-5, with 5 being the highest score.

    c. Any thoughts or feedback about your study guide.

    d. Your first and last name and your mailing address, so we know where to send your free DVD!

Thank you!

LSAT Prep Book
2018-2019

LSAT Prep Books Team

Table of Contents

Test Taking Strategies

1. Reading the Whole Question

A popular assumption in western culture is the idea that we don't have enough time for anything. We speed while driving to work, we want to read an assignment for class as quickly as possible, or we want the line in the supermarket to dwindle faster. However, speeding through such events robs us from being able to thoroughly appreciate and understand what's happening around us. While taking a timed test, the feeling one might have while reading a question is to find the correct answer as quickly as possible. Although pace is important, don't let it deter you from reading the whole question. Test writers know how to subtly change a test question toward the end in various ways, such as adding a negative or changing focus. If the question has a passage, carefully read the whole passage as well before moving on to the questions. This will help you process the information in the passage rather than worrying about the questions you've just read and where to find them. A thorough understanding of the passage or question is an important way for test takers to be able to succeed on an exam.

2. Examining Every Answer Choice

Let's say we're at the market buying apples. The first apple we see on top of the heap may *look* like the best apple, but if we turn it over we can see bruising on the skin. We must examine several apples before deciding which apple is the best. Finding the correct answer choice is like finding the best apple. Some exams ask for the *best* answer choice, which means that there are several choices that could be correct, but one choice is always better than the rest. Although it's tempting to choose an answer that seems correct at first without reading the others, it's important to read each answer choice thoroughly before making a final decision on the answer. The aim of a test writer might be to get as close as possible to the correct answer, so watch out for subtle words that may indicate an answer is incorrect. Once the correct answer choice is selected, read the question again and the answer in response to make sure all your bases are covered.

3. Eliminating Wrong Answer Choices

Sometimes we become paralyzed when we are confronted with too many choices. Which frozen yogurt flavor is the tastiest? Which pair of shoes look the best with this outfit? What type of car will fill my needs as a consumer? If you are unsure of which answer would be the best to choose, it may help to use process of elimination. We use "filtering" all the time on sites such as eBay® or Craigslist® to eliminate the ads that are not right for us. We can do the same thing on an exam. Process of elimination is crossing out the answer choices we know for sure are wrong and leaving the ones that might be correct. It may help to cover up the incorrect answer choices with a piece of paper, although if the exam is computer-based, you may have to use your hand or mentally cross out the incorrect answer choices. Covering incorrect choices is a psychological act that alleviates stress due to the brain being exposed to a smaller amount of information. Choosing between two answer choices is much easier than choosing between four or five, and you have a better chance of selecting the correct answer if you have less to focus on.

4. Sticking to the World of the Question

When we are attempting to answer questions, our minds will often wander away from the question and what it is asking. We begin to see answer choices that are true in the real world instead of true in the world of the question. It may be helpful to think of each test question as its own little world. This world may be different from ours. This world may know as a truth that the chicken came before the egg or may assert that two plus two equals five. Remember that, no matter what hypothetical nonsense may be in the question, assume it to be true. If the question states that the chicken came before the egg, then choose your answer based on that truth. Sticking to the world of the question means placing all of our biases and assumptions aside and relying on the question to guide us to the correct answer. If we are simply looking for answers that are correct based on our own judgment, then we may choose incorrectly. Remember an answer that is true does not necessarily answer the question.

5. Key Words

If you come across a complex test question that you have to read over and over again, try pulling out some key words from the question in order to understand what exactly it is asking. Key words may be words that surround the question, such as *main idea, analogous, parallel, resembles, structured,* or *defines.* The question may be asking for the main idea, or it may be asking you to define something. Deconstructing the sentence may also be helpful in making the question simpler before trying to answer it. This means taking the sentence apart and obtaining meaning in pieces, or separating the question from the foundation of the question. For example, let's look at this question:

Given the author's description of the content of paleontology in the first paragraph, which of the following is most parallel to what it taught?

The question asks which one of the answers most *parallels* the following information: The *description* of paleontology in the first paragraph. The first step would be to see *how* paleontology is described in the first paragraph. Then, we would find an answer choice that parallels that description. The question seems complex at first, but after we deconstruct it, the answer becomes much more attainable.

6. Subtle Negatives

Negative words in question stems will be words such as *not, but, neither,* or *except.* Test writers often use these words in order to trick unsuspecting test takers into selecting the wrong answer—or, at least, to test their reading comprehension of the question. Many exams will feature the negative words in all caps (*which of the following is NOT an example*), but some questions will add the negative word seamlessly into the sentence. The following is an example of a subtle negative used in a question stem:

According to the passage, which of the following is *not* considered to be an example of paleontology?

If we rush through the exam, we might skip that tiny word, *not,* inside the question, and choose an answer that is opposite of the correct choice. Again, it's important to read the question fully, and double check for any words that may negate the statement in any way.

7. Spotting the Hedges

The word "hedging" refers to language that remains vague or avoids absolute terminology. Absolute terminology consists of words like *always, never, all, every, just, only, none,* and *must.* Hedging refers to words like *seem, tend, might, most, some, sometimes, perhaps, possibly, probability,* and *often.* In some cases, we want to choose answer choices that use hedging and avoid answer choices that use absolute terminology. Of course, this always depends on what subject you are being tested on. Humanities subjects like history and literature will contain hedging, because those subjects often do not have absolute answers. However, science and math may contain absolutes that are necessary for the question to be answered. It's important to pay attention to what subject you are on and adjust your response accordingly. In contrast,

8. Restating to Understand

Every now and then we come across questions that we don't understand. The language may be too complex, or the question is structured in a way that is meant to confuse the test taker. When you come across a question like this, it may be worth your time to rewrite or restate the question in your own words in order to understand it better. For example, let's look at the following complicated question:

Which of the following words, if substituted for the word *parochial* in the first paragraph, would LEAST change the meaning of the sentence?

Let's restate the question in order to understand it better. We know that they want the word *parochial* replaced. We also know that this new word would "least" or "not" change the meaning of the sentence. Now let's try the sentence again:

Which word could we replace with *parochial,* and it would not change the meaning?

Restating it this way, we see that the question is asking for a synonym. Now, let's restate the question so we can answer it better:

Which word is a synonym for the word *parochial?*

Before we even look at the answer choices, we have a simpler, restated version of a complicated question. Remember that, if you have paper, you can always rewrite the simpler version of the question so as not to forget it.

9. Guessing

When is it okay to guess on an exam? This question depends on the test format of the particular exam you're taking. On some tests, answer choices that are answered incorrectly are penalized. If you know that you are penalized for wrong answer choices, avoid guessing on the test question. If you can narrow the question down to fifty percent by process of elimination, then perhaps it may be worth it to guess between two answer choices. But if you are unsure of the correct answer choice among three or four answers, it may help to leave the question unanswered. Likewise, if the exam you are taking does *not* penalize for wrong answer choices, answer the questions first you know to be true, then go back through and mark an answer choice, even if you do not know the correct answer. This way, you will at least have a one in four chance of getting the answer correct. It may also be helpful to do some research on the exam you plan to take in order to understand how the questions are graded.

10. Avoiding Patterns

One popular myth in grade school relating to standardized testing is that test writers will often put multiple-choice answers in patterns. A runoff example of this kind of thinking is that the most common answer choice is "C," with "B" following close behind. Or, some will advocate certain made-up word patterns that simply do not exist. Test writers do not arrange their correct answer choices in any kind of pattern; their choices are randomized. There may even be times where the correct answer choice will be the same letter for two or three questions in a row, but we have no way of knowing when or if this might happen. Instead of trying to figure out what choice the test writer probably set as being correct, focus on what the *best answer choice* would be out of the answers you are presented with. Use the tips above, general knowledge, and reading comprehension skills in order to best answer the question, rather than looking for patterns that do not exist.

FREE DVD OFFER

Achieving a high score on your exam depends not only on understanding the content, but also on understanding how to apply your knowledge and your command of test taking strategies. **Because your success is our primary goal, we offer a FREE Study Tips DVD, which provides top-notch test taking strategies to help you optimize your testing experience.**

Our simple request in exchange for the strategy-packed DVD packed is that you email us your feedback about our study guide.

To receive your **FREE Study Tips DVD**, email freedvd@apexprep.com. Please put "FREE DVD" in the subject line and put the following in the email:

a. The name of the study guide you purchased.

b. Your rating of the study guide on a scale of 1-5, with 5 being the highest score.

c. Any thoughts or feedback about your study guide.

d. Your first and last name and your mailing address, so we know where to send your free DVD!

Introduction to the LSAT

Function of the Test

The Law School Admission Test (LSAT) is a required component of the application process to nearly all law schools in the United States that are accredited by the American Board Association (ABA). There may be other unaccredited law schools and a few accredited ones that accept GRE scores instead of LSAT scores, but for all intents and purposes, LSAT scores are necessary for consideration of admission to all Juris Doctor (JD) programs in the country. Accordingly, nearly all test takers are prospective candidates for JD programs in in the United States, Canada, and certain other countries.

The test is designed and administered by the Law School Admission Council (LSAC). Like the SAT, GRE, and other standardized tests used primarily for the admissions process to educational institutions, the LSAT does not have a set "passing score." Instead, minimum scores and the importance of the score (its weight) in deciding a candidate's acceptance into the program is determined by each individual law program. Scores are typically considered alongside other criteria such as courses taken, GPA, personal recommendations, among other things.

Although the LSAT is a prerequisite for nearly all accredited programs in the United States, the number of LSAT exams administered annually has dropped by nearly 40% since the 2009-2010 academic year. The LSAC reports that score distributions, which follow a normal bell curve, remain very stable from year to year.

Test Administration

There are four dates per academic year on which the LSAT is offered. The test is typically administered on a Saturday in September, December, February, and June. Alternative Monday dates are usually offered exclusively for those who cannot attend a Saturday administration for religious reasons. There are hundreds of available testing locations around the United States, Canada, and many other countries; however, the dates may vary, and these international testing sites may offer fewer than four administration dates during the academic year.

It is recommended that candidates register for the exam on or before the posted deadlines in order to optimize the chances of receiving their preferred date and location. Registration can be completed online, by submitting a paper registration form, or by phone. At the time of registration, the test fee must be paid. In addition to the base fee for the exam, additional fees are incurred for late registrations, location changes, requests for hand scoring, and other potential changes or services.

The LSAC offers a variety of accommodations for test takers with documented disabilities. It is important to note that a candidate seeking accommodations must register for the LSAT first before submitting documentation in support of his or her disabilities. Registration must be completed prior to the deadline in order to request accommodations. The necessary forms and materials are available on the LSAC website (https://www.lsac.org/jd/lsat/accommodated-testing).

Test Format

There are five thirty-five-minute sections comprised of multiple-choice questions on the LSAT. Four of the sections—a Reading Comprehension section, an Analytical Reasoning section, and two Logical Reasoning sections—are scored, and one section—the "variable" section—is unscored. This variable section contains material that the test developers are testing out for consideration on future exams. While taking the exam, test takers are not informed about which section contains the unscored, pretest questions, though this information is divulged on the score report. Following the conclusion of these five sections, there is an unscored thirty-five-minute writing sample section. The writing completed during the allotted time is sent to the law schools to which the candidate applies.

The LSAT is administered in a paper test booklet. Test takers must use a No. 2 pencil (mechanical pencils of any type are not allowed) and complete the test by hand. It is recommended that test takers bring an extra eraser and a manual pencil sharpener. All items must be contained in a clear plastic sealable bag, no larger than one-gallon capacity. A list of permissible items is available on the LSAC website (https://www.lsac.org/jd/help/faqs-lsat).

Scoring

A candidate's raw score on the LSAT is calculated by totaling the number of questions that he or she answered correctly. All sections and questions are weighted equally. Incorrect responses are not penalized, so the test taker incurs no risk by guessing. A test taker's raw score is then scaled to the standard LSAT score from 120 to 180. This scaling process accounts for differences in difficulty between test forms and allows scores to be compared.

Although there is no set passing score, obtaining high scores is important for candidates seeking admission to competitive law programs. The typical LSAT score for a student accepted to a moderately competitive law school hovers around 145 or 150, while the most competitive law schools are usually looking for LSAT scores of 165 or higher. Although candidates can retake the test a couple of times, schools receive all grades and often take the average score into consideration rather than the highest score. There is also a risk of receiving a lower score on a retest, and since schools will also receive this score, candidates should be judicious in their decisions to retake the LSAT.

LSAT Logical Reasoning

The LSAT contains two Logical Reasoning sections, both with 25 questions, so this section comprises a significant portion of the test. The questions in the Logical Reasoning section of the LSAT evaluate the test taker's ability to critically consider, analyze, and complete various arguments presented in common language. These skills are paramount to the success of a law student and future attorney, who must develop a strong foundation of critical reasoning skills. Lawyers are constantly tasked with evaluating, analyzing, building, and refuting arguments and identifying gaps, inconsistencies, fallacies, and assumptions in such arguments.

The LSAT test developers design the arguments and their associated questions in the Logical Reasoning section to require the same type of legal reasoning that prospective law students will encounter in their studies and careers. Rather than using legalese and law as a subject matter, for the most part, questions are based on short arguments that address ordinary situations in common language, such as those found in newspapers, academic publications, advertisements, media of various kinds, and magazines.

It is useful for test takers to bear in mind that the questions on the LSAT do not require specialized outside knowledge. For example, even if the argument addresses the viability of renewable energy sources, the test taker does not need prior background in energy sources to successfully answer the question. The LSAT is designed to specifically assess how one considers and analyzes premises, not their familiarity with particular subject matter. In fact, it is important for test takers to avoid viewing the concepts in the argument in the context of their own prior knowledge, opinions, or beliefs. Instead, they should only consider the closed system of the presented argument and associated question.

The exercises in the Logical Reasoning not only contain sufficient information to correctly answer the questions, but they also allow test takers to determine which part of the question (the argument or the provided answer choices) should be assumed to be "true" and used as the benchmark against which the other part should be evaluated. The question stem in a Logical Reasoning question can potentially establish one of two different relationships between the argument and the provided answer choices: either the argument is stated as truth and the answer choices are evaluated in accordance to it, or each of the five answer choices are asserted as truths, and the positive or negative effect of each choice on the argument must be evaluated.

Recognizing Parts of an Argument and Their Relationships

Premise and Conclusion
Not all arguments on the LSAT Logical Reasoning section are true "arguments"; some are merely collections of factual statements strung together. For this reason, some texts use the term *stimulus* to describe the text part of a problem that precedes the question and answer choices, as *argument* can be a misnomer.

Stimuli that are true arguments contain a *conclusion* that is derived from statements called *premises*, which give reasons why whatever is asserted in the conclusion should be believed. For example, consider the following simple argument:

> All basketball players are tall. Christopher is a basketball player. Therefore, Christopher is tall.

In this short argument, the first two statements provide the reasons to accept the third statement. Thus, the premises are: *All basketball players are tall,* and *Christopher is a basketball player.* The conclusion is: *Christopher is tall.*

It is worth mentioning again that some arguments presented on the LSAT may contain factual inaccuracies or opinions that test takers disagree with. The LSAT test developers purposely design certain exercises in this manner to try and trip up test takers who draw upon their own knowledge, common sense, or experience. It is important to remember that the test is evaluating one's ability to reason logically and use provided "evidence," rather than assess their opinions and subject area expertise.

Assumption

In the structure of an argument, an *assumption* is an unstated premise. Many Logical Reasoning questions will ask you to identify the assumption within arguments, and you must find something that the argument is relying on that the author is not stating explicitly. Many strengthening and weakening questions deal with unstated assumptions, as well as necessary and sufficient assumption questions. Let's take a look at what an unsated assumption looks like:

> All restaurants in the Seattle area serve vegan food. *Haile's Seafood* must serve vegan food.

Let's identify all parts of the argument, including the unstated assumption. The conclusion of this argument is the last sentence: *Haile's Seafood* must serve vegan food. The premise we are given is the first sentence: All restaurants in the Seattle area serve vegan food. Now let's ask ourselves if there's a missing link. How did the author reach this conclusion? The author reached this conclusion with an unstated assumption, which might look like this: *Haile's Seafood* is in the Seattle area. Now we have the argument:

> Premise: All restaurants in the Seattle area serve vegan food.

> Unstated Assumption: *Haile's Seafood* is in the Seattle area.

> Conclusion: *Haile's Seafood* must serve vegan food

Another way to look at the missing link is like this: there is a connection between "Seattle area" and "vegan food," and one between *"Haile's Seafood"* and "vegan food", but there is no connection between "Seattle area" and *"Haile's Seafood."* The unstated assumption identifies this connection.

Fact Sets

Stimuli that are fact sets rather than arguments contain a group of statements but lack any sort of conclusion. For example, consider the following fact set:

There are three elementary schools in town. Fort River has 240 students. Wildwood has 275 students. Crocker Farm has 180 students.

An argument, by definition, must include a conclusion; therefore, the prior four sentences do not constitute an argument, because no conclusion is presented. Instead, the statements simply assert facts about the elementary schools without inflicting judgement or answering *so what?* One useful tip for test takers to determine whether the stimulus contains an argument or a fact set is to evaluate, on a very basic level, whether they feel a reaction after reading. Fact sets, by nature, do not evoke much of an emotional response and read more like a list of assertions with no obvious "point." Arguments, on the other hand, often draw readers in more, causing them to "care," question, disagree, or otherwise evoke some sort of emotional reaction.

Again, arguments must contain a conclusion, which is a judgement or statement that the author wants readers to believe given one or multiple reasons (premises) that serve as evidence or tools to persuade the readers to accept the conclusion. The conclusion is commonly signaled by words such as *so, therefore, thus, for this reason, accordingly, hence, shows that, consequently, as a result*, etc. Words that are commonly indicative of premises include *because, for, since, in order to, for example, as indicated by, owing to, due to, this is evidenced by*, etc. While premises and conclusions are often signaled by these words and phrases, they do not always include such explicit indicators.

When stimuli are true arguments, it is critical to identify the conclusion prior to considering the answer choices to the question because the crux of the question often lies in the conclusion. Failing to fully grasp and mentally consider the conclusion can cause unfocused test takers to fall for red herrings or answer choices purposely designed to contain just small inaccuracies or inconsistencies from the conclusion or premises.

Patterns of Reasoning

One of the question types in the Logical Reasoning section of the LSAT exam will ask about patterns of reasoning. Patterns of reasoning involve deconstructing an argument and putting general terms to each of the steps involved. Then, it is up to the test taker to apply those general terms to another specific argument. The following is an example of a question stem involving patterns of reasoning:

Cassandra will go to the auto repair shop this evening only if Bobby goes to the tire store. Bobby won't go to the tire store unless Sara agrees to go to the tire store. However, Sara refuses to go to the tire store. Therefore, Cassandra will not go to the auto repair shop this evening.

The pattern of reasoning in which one of the following arguments is most similar to that in the argument above?

> a. If Laura goes on vacation, it is highly unlikely that Mercedes will buy a car this evening. Laura will not go on vacation unless she finds someone to water her plants. Laura has found someone to water her plants, so Mercedes will not buy a car this evening.
> b. Sam will mow the grass this morning only if Juan goes to the movies. Juan won't go to the movies unless Braxton agrees to enroll in college. Therefore, Sam will mow the grass this morning.
> c. Katie will start on her painting only if Catarina does not play in her soccer tournament today. Since Catarina ended up getting hurt, she cannot play in her soccer tournament, so Katie will start on her painting today.
> d. Jackson will do the dishes tomorrow only if Maria goes to school. Maria will not have to go to school unless Jake is sick. Since Jake is not sick, Jackson will not do the dishes tomorrow.
> e. Billie can go to the auto repair shop if Vicky goes to the tire store. Vicky won't go to the tire store unless Samson agrees to go to the tire store. However, it is highly unlikely that Samson will agree to go to the tire store. Therefore, Billie will most likely not go to the auto repair shop.

Let's find out what the logical structure of this argument is. For visual learners, it may help to draw a diagram of the logical sequence of statements. For now, we can see the following:

> Cassandra @ auto shop → Bobby @ tire store

Remember, though, that Bobby will go to the tire store only if Sara goes. So, we have:

> Cassandra @ auto shop → Bobby @ tire store → Sara to tire store

Since we know the information on who did what, the chain looks like this in its reasoning:

Cassandra no auto shop → Bobby no tire store → Sara no tire store

Since Sara refuses to go to the tire store, Bobby will not go to the tire store. Since Bobby will not go to the tire store, then Cassandra will not go to the auto shop. The pattern of reasoning that relates to this stem the most is Choice *D*.

Jackson no dishes → Maria no school → Jake not sick

We see that the pattern is the same as in the question stem. Even the language looks the same. We see the conditional statements mirroring each other (if → then). Here are what the other patterns look like:

Choice A
Mercedes highly unlikely car → Laura @ vacation → Stranger @ plants

In Choice *A* we are hit with the language of "highly unlikely," which we do not see in the original question stem. Mark this one as incorrect.

Choice B
Sam @ grass → Juan movies → Braxton ? college

In Choice *B*, we are missing a key ingredient toward the end of the statement. We're going to assume that Braxton probably enrolled in college since Sam ended up mowing the grass. However, since we are not told this information for sure, then the pattern of reasoning is different from that in the stem.

Choice C
Katie @ painting → Catarina no soccer tournament

In Choice *C*, we see that the pattern is off because we only have two people in the pattern instead of three. Pay attention to the number of constituents within the pattern as well as the language used to express the pattern.

Choice E
Billie unlikely to auto repair store → Vicky probably not tire store → Samson highly unlikely tire store.

Again, pay attention to the language. The language in this choice is not conditional statements (if → then). Instead, the language is unsure of what each entity will do. What's tricky about this choice is that it deals with the same destinations. However, since the language within the pattern is different, it is incorrect.

Drawing Well-Supported Conclusions

The conclusion question types in the Logical Reasoning section presents evidence within the stimulus and asks test takers to draw a conclusion from that evidence. Some of the conclusion question types will ask what test takers can "infer," "imply," or "conclude" from the given information. Other language used in conclusion questions might consist of the following:

- Must also be true
- Provide the most support for
- Which one of the following conclusions

- Most strongly supported by
- Properly inferred

Making inferences and drawing conclusions involve skills that are quite similar: both require readers to fill in information the test writer has omitted. To make an inference or draw a conclusion about the text, test takers should observe all facts and arguments the test writer has presented. The best way to understand ways to drawing well-supported conclusions is by practice. Let's take a look at the following example:

Nutritionist: More and more bodybuilders each year turn to whey protein as a source for their supplement intake to repair muscle tissue after working out. More and more studies are showing that using whey as a source of protein is linked to prostate cancer in men. Bodybuilders who use whey protein may consider switching to a plant-based protein source in order to avoid developing the negative effects that come with whey protein consumption.

Which of the following most accurately expresses the conclusion of the nutritionist's argument?

> a. Whey protein is an excellent way to repair muscles after a workout.
> b. Bodybuilders should switch from whey to a plant-based protein.
> c. Whey protein causes every single instance of prostate cancer in men.
> d. We still don't know the causes of prostate cancer in men.
> e. It's possible that bodybuilding may cause prostate cancer.

The correct answer choice is *B*: bodybuilders should switch from whey to a plant-based protein. We can gather this from the entirety of the passage, as it begins with what kind of protein bodybuilders consume, the dangers of that protein, and what kind of protein to switch to. Choice *A* is incorrect; this is the opposite of what the passage states. When reading through answer choices, it's important to look for choices that include the words "every," "always," or "all." In many instances, absolute answer choices will not be the correct answer. This example is shown in Choice *C*; the passage does not state that whey protein causes "every single instance" of prostate cancer in men, only that it is *linked* to prostate cancer in men. Choice *D* is incorrect; although the nutritionist doesn't list all the causes of prostate cancer in men, the nutritionist does not conclude that we don't know the causes of prostate cancer in men either. Finally, Choice *E* is incorrect. This answer choice makes a jump from bodybuilding to prostate cancer, which is incorrect. The passage states that bodybuilders consume more whey protein, which is linked to cancer, not that bodybuilding *itself* causes cancer.

The key to drawing well-supported conclusions is to read the question stem in its entirety a few times over and then paraphrase the passage in your own words. Once you do this, you will get an idea of the passage's conclusion before you are confused by all the different answer choices. Remember that drawing a conclusion is different than making an assumption. With drawing a conclusion, we are relying solely on the passage for facts to come to our conclusion. Making an assumption goes beyond the facts of the passage, so be careful of answer choices depicting assumptions instead of passage-based conclusions.

Reasoning by Analogy

Analogy questions in the Logical Reasoning section of the LSAT exam are very common. In its most basic definition, an *analogy* is a comparison between two things. Lawyers use reasoning by analogy frequently in their professional careers in order to compare past successful cases with present cases they are trying to argue. For analogy questions, there are several specific question types you will run into:

Flawed Reasoning

For analogies in flawed reasoning questions, many people make the mistake of assuming that the two things being compared *are alike in every respect*. If they are not, it is flawed reasoning by analogy. Let's look at an example at a faulty analogy in a flawed reasoning question:

Mary Oliver is a great poet, and she practices writing every single day. Therefore, if I practice writing every single day, I will be a great poet.

The example above is flawed because it assumes that Mary Oliver and I are the same in every respect. Perhaps she received a better education than me, and that is why she is a great poet. Or maybe her father was a poet and taught her everything she needed to know to be a great poet. The possibilities are endless as to why this analogy does not work out.

Necessary Assumption

We will talk in depth about necessary assumption later, but for the sake of necessary assumption dealing with analogy, let's use the same example above. A necessary assumption means that at least one thing *must be required* in order for the argument to be true. Here is a proper answer to a necessary assumption question dealing with analogy:

Mary Oliver practices writing, and her practice causes her to become a stronger writer. Therefore, if I practice writing every day, I will become a stronger writer.

What is an assumption on which this argument relies?

All humans that practice writing will get better due to the neurological structure of the brain and how the brain responds to that practice.

For necessary assumption, we want to look at how the two entities are similar *in at least one aspect*. We see here that, at the very least, Mary Oliver and I are both human, and that our brains will respond similarly to practice, leading to stronger writing.

Sufficient Assumption

Again, we will go into more depth on sufficient assumption questions later, but let's look at these types of questions dealing with analogies. For a sufficient assumption, we want the two entities to be alike *in all related respects*.

Mary Oliver practices writing, and her practice causes her to become a stronger writer. Therefore, if I practice writing every day, I will become a stronger writer.

Which of the following, if assumed, allows the conclusion to be drawn properly?

Every human responds in the same way when they practice writing.

Whether this is true in real life or not, we have a valid argument with this sufficient assumption question. Analogies in the sufficient assumption context tell us that Mary Oliver and I are the same in every way when we practice writing; therefore, my assertion to become a stronger writer is totally valid.

Recognizing Misunderstandings or Points of Disagreement

On the LSAT, some question stems will have two separate passages addressing a similar topic. Both passages will be spoken by someone like a scientist, politician, or doctor, or it might even just be someone's last name, like "Rodriguez" or "Powell." The two passages are meant to disagree with or misunderstand each other. The question will usually ask a "point at issue" between the two speakers, or how the two speakers disagree in the passages. The answer explanations will try to throw in choices that relate to the topic but ones the speakers do not have opinions on. Watch out for these, as they are only meant to confuse you. Regarding the choices, ask yourself, first and foremost, does either speaker have an opinion on this statement? And if no opinion is expressed in the original passage, mark the answer as incorrect. Let's look at an example of a Point at Issue question:

Jones: Our company's decision to change driving routes may have been detrimental to the company. The new route is longer by half an hour, which cuts down the efficiency of when the goods get delivered, which, in turn, makes us lose money.

Martinez: The newer, updated route was the best decision. The old route had safety hazards for truck drivers. The newer route will cut down on accidents, which will make up for the cost of delivering the goods later.

A point of issue between Jones and Martinez is whether

> a. the new driving route will save the company money.
> b. the old driving route is safer than the new driving route.
> c. the company will go bankrupt due to this change in route.
> d. the shipment will make it on time via the new route.
> e. the goods are too expensive and should be lowered.

The correct answer choice is *A*. Jones and Martinez disagree over whether the new driving route will save the company money. Choice *B* is incorrect; although Martinez admits that the new route is safer than the old route, Jones has no opinion on safety, which makes this choice incorrect. Choice *C* is incorrect; neither of the speakers mention the company's potential to go bankrupt. In Choice *D*, Jones is worried about shipments making it on time, but Martinez is not concerned with time here; Martinez is more concerned with safety. Finally, Choice *E* is incorrect; neither speaker worries about the price of the goods. When reading the answer choices, make sure each speaker has an opinion concerning the one you choose. Here, we see both speakers mention money saved, so Choice *A* is the correct answer choice.

Determining How Additional Evidence Affects an Argument

Questions seeking evidence that most undermines or weakens the argument require test takers to read the stated premises in the argument and ask themselves what must be assumed true, but is not explicitly stated in the provided premises, in order for the argument to jump to its conclusion. The correct answer choice most directly contradicts, rules out, or refutes the identified unstated assumption or missing link. Questions seeking evidence that most strengthens or supports the argument require a similar approach with test takers considering the same question as they read the argument. Once the assumption is identified, they should review the answer choices for the one that most directly affirms or presents that missing link. First, let's take a look at a weakening question below:

New electronic watches called "LiteBites" promise to track the fitness goals of whomever purchases them. The sales have increased in the past year. Although these watches have been extremely popular for a decade since they came out, this popularity is expected to recede from here on out, due to the fact that the age group purchasing these watches, ages 16 to 25, is expected to decline over the next ten years.

Which of the following, if true, would most seriously weaken the argument?

   a. A new fitness watch called "TrackIt" came out this year.
   b. Everyone should get a "LiteBite" for health and wellness purposes.
   c. "LiteBite" watches have gotten negative reviews this year.
   d. The new "LiteBite" model is now waterproof.
   e. Most "LiteBite" sales in the past year have been from adults 25 years or older.

The correct answer choice will find an unstated assumption of the passage and attack it. An assumption in the passage is that the age group from 16 to 25 are the ones responsible for the recent one-year increase in sales. Choice *E* attacks this assumption, and says that in fact, most LiteBite sales in the past year have been from adults 25 years or older, which completely destroys the argument in question. The rest of the answer choices may explain why the popularity is receding (a new watch came out and negative reviews), but they don't attack the main conclusion of the argument—that adults between 16 and 25 are purchasing them. Choice *E* attacks the central assumption of the passage.

The following is an example of a strengthening argument:

Sandblast is a Norwegian company that makes computers, and Sandblast computers can run for twenty-four hours without having to charge them. Iberion is also a Norwegian company that makes computers; therefore, Iberion computers should also run for twenty-four hours without having to charge them.

The author's argument would be best supported by which one of the following, if that statement were true?

   a. Swedish computers also have the same amount of battery life as Norwegian computers.
   b. All Norwegian computer companies use the same types of batteries in their computers.
   c. The Iberion company focuses on manufacturing computers used specifically for commercial purposes.
   d. Iberion has been making computers for approximately fifteen years.
   e. All Norwegian computer companies have excellent customer service reviews.

First, let's look at the premise and the conclusion. The premise states that Sandblast computers are Norwegian and can run for twenty-four hours on battery and that Iberion computers are also Norwegian. Therefore, Iberion computers should also run for twenty-four hours on battery. Choice *B* is the correct answer because it displays the *similarities* between Sandblast and Iberion: they are both Norwegian and therefore both use the same batteries in their computers. Choices that have irrelevant information are Choices *A*, *D*, and *E*. Choice *C* tells us what the Iberion company focuses on; however, we do not receive information on how this compares to Sandblast computers. Therefore, Choice *B* is the correct answer. If Norwegian companies put the same batteries in all of their computers, then it is likely that Sandblast computers and Iberion computers will run on battery power for a similar amount of time.

Detecting Assumptions Made by Particular Arguments

In the questions directly seeking an unstated assumption, test takers should read the stated premises in the argument and ask themselves what must be assumed true—but that is not explicitly stated in the provided premises—in order for the argument to jump to its conclusion. The correct answer choice will best present that missing link. Here's what assumption questions look like:

- Which of the following, if true, enables the conclusion to be properly drawn?
- The conclusion above is properly drawn if which of the following is assumed?
- The conclusion above follows logically if which one of the following is assumed?
- The argument makes which one of the following assumptions?
- Which of the following is an assumption upon which the argument relies?

Necessary Assumption

Some questions will deal with necessary assumptions, and some questions will deal with sufficient assumptions. Necessary assumptions are assumptions that have to be true in order for the conclusion to hold up. Remember that the basic argument structure goes from premise to conclusion. A necessary assumption is a statement in the middle of the premise and conclusion that is needed in order for the argument to not fall apart. Really, a necessary assumption is an unstated premise in the argument. Necessary assumption questions will use the words "required," "depends," or "relies." Let's look at a necessary assumption example:

Alachua County in Florida has reported no traces of manatees in their river systems from their recent surveys. If there were any manatees present, the surveys would have definitely detected them. Because no manatees were detected, we must conclude that they are extinct.

What is an assumption on which this argument relies?

a. Manatees have been on the verge of extinction before, in the 1990s.
b. The water this year in the river system has been colder than usual.
c. Manatees do not exist anywhere outside of the Alachua County river system.
d. Surveys are becoming more and more accurate for environmental research.
e. Alachua County has also been seeing a decline in gators in the rivers.

Choice *C* is the correct answer choice. Again, a necessary assumption is an unstated premise on which the argument relies. One way to tell if you are choosing the right answer is to negate the answer choice. If we negated the answer choice and the conclusion falls apart, we have chosen the correct answer. Let's negate it: Manatees *do* exist outside of the Alachua County river system. Thus, our argument falls apart, because that means that manatees are in fact *not* extinct. This argument is relying on the fact that manatees *do not* exist outside of the Alachua County river system, thus it is a necessary assumption.

Just for fun, let's negate the rest of the answer choices and see if our argument is destroyed. Choice *A*: If we see manatees have *not* been on the verge of extinction before, would that change the fact that they are on the verge of extinction now? Nope. Choice *B*: The water this year in the river systems has *not* been colder than usual. This does not destroy our conclusion that manatees are extinct. Choice *D*: Surveys are *not* becoming more and more accurate for environmental research. No, this does not destroy our argument, although it does wobble it a little. But for necessary assumption, remember that it must obliterate our conclusion, which *D* does not do. Choice *E*: Alachua County has *not* been seeing a decline in gators in the river. This has nothing to do with manatees, so we can mark it as incorrect.

Sufficient Assumption

Sufficient assumption questions are also known as "justify" questions on the LSAT, although the question stem will rarely contain the word "justify." Sufficient assumption stems present an argument that is not a whole argument. For sufficient assumption questions, we want to look for an answer choice with information that validates the argument. Remember how necessary assumption questions will contain the words "depends," "relies," and "requires"? Sufficient assumption questions will look like the following, often containing words like "Follows logically if . . . assumed," "Properly inferred if . . . assumed," "enables," or "allows." Here are some full sufficient assumption statements:

- Which of the following, if assumed, allows the conclusion to be drawn properly?
- The conclusion follows the premise logically if which of the following is assumed?
- The conclusion is properly inferred if which of the following is assumed?

Telling apart necessary assumption from sufficient assumption is kind of difficult. In a nutshell, here is what each of them is asking:

- Sufficient assumption questions ask you to find an assumption that guarantees the validity of the conclusion; it's like finding the missing piece of a puzzle.

- Necessary assumption questions ask you to find an assumption in the argument that has to be true in order for the argument's logical reasoning to have a chance at being true.

Let's look at an example of a sufficient assumption question:

If the adjuster can't make it out to Jacqueline's property by September 15 or an alternate adjuster cannot be found, her family will not be able to go on their cruise to the Bahamas. An alternative adjuster is out of the question because Jacqueline's insurance will only cover this one specific adjuster. Therefore, Jacqueline and her family will not be able to go to the Bahamas.

The conclusion follows the premise logically if which of the following is assumed?

a. Jacqueline should switch insurance companies; a good insurance company will always provide an alternate adjuster.
b. The adjuster is not available to visit before September 15 because of the chaos relating to the most recent disaster in Hurricane Andy.
c. The adjuster will be available on September 7th through 9th, and they are able to go to Jacqueline's property and look around.
d. In recent years, the Bahamas has become a tourist trap and is no longer seen as the paradise it once was.
e. Jacqueline and her family are lucky to have insurance on their home, as most people will experience natural disasters without insurance to help them afterward.

Choice B is the correct answer. The argument says if the adjuster can't make it out by September 15 or an alternate adjuster can't be found, then the family cannot go to the Bahamas. We see that an alternate adjuster cannot be found. Ok, great. But what about the other condition? Can an adjuster make it out by September 15? The passage does not tell us, so we must look for this information in the answers. Choice B validates the conclusion because it tells us that no, an adjuster cannot get to Jacqueline's house by the 15th. Let's look at the argument in abstract terms:

If Not X and Not Y, then Z. Not Y, Therefore Z.

We are looking for this:

If Not X and Not Y, then Z. Not X and Not Y, Therefore, Z.

In the abstract statement above, the "Not X" is the statement that must be assumed in order for the conclusion to be true. Let's look at the rest of the answer choices:

Choice *A* is incorrect; this tells us what Jacqueline should do in the future and does not give any indication of validating the conclusion—that Jacqueline and her family will not make it to the Bahamas. Choice *C* is incorrect; if this assumption were true, our conclusion would be invalid. We are looking for assumptions that *validate* our conclusion. If the adjuster is able to come, then Jacqueline's family *would* be able to go to the Bahamas, and the conclusion is that they *are not able* to go to the Bahamas. Choice *D* is incorrect; this is information outside of the argument and has no relevance to the conclusion. Choice *E* is incorrect; whether or not we assume this information to be true, that Jacqueline is "lucky" to have insurance, the conclusion is not validated because of it. Mark this choice as incorrect.

Identifying and Applying Principles or Rules

Principle questions on the LSAT logical reasoning portion of the exam are similar to other question types in that they deal with parallel reasoning questions, strengthening questions, and weakening questions, among others. Principle questions, however, use more general concepts to set up questions rather than specific situations. A principle is a fundamental truth that serves for a basis of reasoning or a belief system. Basically, principles offer a direction to what one should or should not do in a given situation. On the LSAT, it's important to remember that the world of the question is always true, regardless of whether it is true in real life. Therefore, principle questions on the LSAT must be accepted as true, no matter what logic or "real life" tells us.

Principle questions will have different scenarios in the question stem. The questions asked may be one of the following:

- Which one of the general principles most supports the argument above?
- The situation described above most closely conforms to which of the following principles?
- The argument above most closely conforms to which of the following generalizations?
- Which one of the following principles, if valid, most helps to justify the decision above?

Here is an example of a principle question:

> In the 1990's, DEA agent Sandra O'Neal's primary purpose was to catch the largest cocaine traffickers coming in and out of Colombia. The problem with this scenario was that O'Neal had to work with an alternate cartel in order to catch the biggest and most dangerous cartel: Medellín. DEA agent Herald Luego fought O'Neal with this decision and tried everything he could to stop her from "getting in bed with the devil." To O'Neal, her actions were justified when they caught the leader of the Medellín cartel. However, Luego still disagrees with the tactics to this day.

Agent Herald Luego's ideas about drug enforcement pertaining to Sandra O'Neal most closely conforms to which of the following principles?

a. The good of the majority is always the best outcome.
b. If a person repents of a crime, he or she deserves mercy.
c. Do unto others as you would have them do unto you.
d. A favorable outcome does not excuse crimes committed to achieve it.
e. Above all, one must respect personal privacy.

We see that the moral principle that Agent Herald Luego most likely conforms to is answer choice *D:* a favorable outcome does not excuse crimes committed to achieve it. Luego does not agree with O'Neal's actions to catch the main cartel, because her means to catch this cartel are morally corrupt, and thus do not justify the end result. Luego's principles would assert that everything to catch the main cartel is done by the book, no matter what, because of what his principles state. For principle questions, if one upholds a certain principle, they must make up their mind to enforce that principle in whatever situation. Choice *A* would most likely align with Agent O'Neal's principles: the good of the majority is always the best outcome, so this is incorrect. Choices *B*, *C*, and *D* do not apply to this particular situation.

Identifying Flaws in Arguments

In some question stems, the LSAT test designers will ask you to identify some type of flaw in an argument's reasoning. The question is not really asking for information to strengthen or weaken the statement, or an assumption to validate the conclusion, like the strengthen, weaken, or assumption questions. Rather, argument flaw questions want you to provide a description of that error. In order for you to be able to describe what flaw is occurring in the argument, it will help to know of various argumentative flaws, such as red herring, false choice, and correlation vs. causation. We will look at those below. Here are some examples of what Flaw Questions look like:

- The reasoning in the argument is flawed because the argument . . .
- The argument is most vulnerable to criticism on the grounds that it . . .
- Which one of the following is an error in the argument's reasoning?
- A flaw in the reasoning of the argument is that . . .
- Which one of the following most accurately describes X's criticism of the argument made by Y?

Bait/Switch
One common flaw that is good to know is called the "bait and switch." It occurs when the test makers will provide an argument that offers evidence about X, and ends the argument with a conclusion about Y. A "bait and switch" answer choice will look like this:

> The argument assumes that X does in fact address Y without providing justification.

Let's look at an example:

> Hannah will most likely always work out and maintain a healthy physique. After all, Hannah's IQ is extremely high.

The correct answer will look like this:

> The argument assumes that Hannah's high IQ addresses her likelihood of always working out without providing justification.

Ascriptive Error
The ascriptive argument will begin the argument with something a third party has claimed. Usually, it will be something very general, like "Some people say that . . ." or "Generally, it has been said . . ." Then, the arguer will follow up that claim with a refutation or opposing view. The problem here is that when the arguer phrases something in this general sense without a credible source, their refutation of that evidence doesn't really matter. Here's an example:

It has been said that peppermint oil has been proven to relieve stomach issues and, in some cases, prevent cancer. I can attest to the relief in stomach issues; however, there is just not enough evidence to prove whether or not peppermint oil has the ability to prevent any kind of cancerous cells from forming in the body.

The correct answer will look like this:

> The argument assumes that the refuting evidence matters to the position that is being challenged.
>
> We have no credible source in this argument, so the refutation is senseless.

Prescriptive Error

First, let's take a look at what "prescriptive" means. Prescriptive means to give directions, or to say something *ought to* or *should* do something else. On the LSAT, sometimes an argument will be a descriptive premise (simply describing) that leads to a prescriptive conclusion, which makes for a very weak argument. This is like saying "There is a hurricane coming; therefore, we should leave the state." Even though this seems like common sense, the logical soundness of this argument is missing. A valid argument is when the truth of the premise leads absolutely to the truth of the conclusion. It's when the conclusion *is* something, not when the conclusion *should* be or do something. The flaw here is the assumption that the conclusion is going to work out; something prescriptive is not ever guaranteed to work out in a logical argument.

False Choice

A false choice, or false dilemma, flaw on the LSAT is a statement that assumes only the object it lists in the statement is the solution, or the only options that exist, for that problem. Here is an example:

> I didn't get the grade I want in Chemistry class. I must either be really stupid, I didn't get enough sleep, or I didn't eat enough that day.

This is a false choice error. We are offered only three options for why the speaker did not get the grade he or she wanted in Chemistry class. However, there is potentially more options why the grade was not achieved other than the three listed. The speaker could have been fighting a cold, or the professor may not have taught the material in a comprehensive way. It is our job as test takers to recognize that there are more options other than the choices we are given, although it appears that the only three choices are listed in the example.

Red Herring

A red herring is a point offered in an argument that is only meant to distract or mislead. A red herring will throw something out after the argument that is unrelated to the argument, although it still commands attention, thus taking attention away from the relevant issue. The following is an example of a red herring fallacy:

Kirby: It seems like therapy is moving toward a more holistic model rather than something prescriptive, where the space between a therapist and client is seen more organic rather than a controlled space. This helps empower the client to reach their own conclusions about what should be done rather than having someone tell them what to do.

Barlock: What's the point of therapy anyway? It seems like "talking out" problems with a stranger is a waste of time and always has been. Is it even successful as a profession?

We see Kirby present an argument about the route therapy is taking toward the future. Instead of responding to the argument by presenting their own side regarding where therapy is headed, Barlock questions the overall point of therapy. Barlock throws out a red herring here: Kirby cannot proceed with the argument because now Kirby must defend the existence of therapy instead of its future.

Correlation Versus Causality

The LSAT test developers frequently make use of cause-and-effect reasoning in arguments to explain why something has or has not occurred. Test takers should be careful when reviewing causal conclusions because the reasoning is often flawed, incorrectly classifying correlation as causality. In many Logical Reasoning arguments (as well as real-world situations), two events that may or may not be associated with one another are said to be linked such that one was the cause or reason for the other, which is considered the effect. To be a true "cause-and-effect" relationship, one factor or event must occur first (the cause) and be the sole reason (unless others are also listed) that the other occurred (the effect). The cause serves as the initiator of the relationship between the two events.

For example, consider the following argument:

> Last weekend, the local bakery ran out of blueberry muffins and some customers had to select something else instead. This week, the bakery's sales have fallen. Therefore, the blueberry muffin shortage last weekend resulted in fewer sales this week.

In this argument, the author states that the decline in sales this week (the effect) was caused by the shortage of blueberry muffins last weekend. However, there are other viable alternate causes for the decline in sales this week besides the blueberry muffin shortage. Perhaps it is summer and many normal patrons are away this week on vacation, or maybe another local bakery just opened or is running a special sale this week. There might be a large construction project or road work in town near the bakery, deterring customers from navigating the detours or busy roads. It is entirely possible that the decline this week is just a random coincidence and not attributable to any factor other than chance, and that next week, sales will return to normal or even exceed typical sales. Insufficient evidence exists to confidently assert that the blueberry muffin shortage was the sole reason for the decline in sales, thus mistaking correlation for causation.

Identifying Explanations

Explanation questions are another kind of question type on the LSAT Logical Reasoning section. Note that these are interchangeable for "Paradox Questions" or "Discrepancy Questions." Explanation questions ask you to find an explanation for one thing in particular, or for something that seems paradoxical. First, it's helpful to designate what the paradox or phenomenon is in the question stem. Then, you must look for the answer that best explains or resolves the phenomenon in a logical way. The following examples are what explanation questions look like:

- Which one of the following, if true, most helps to explain the difference . . .?
- Which one of the following, if true, will resolve the discrepancy above?
- Which of the following, if true, most helps to explain the phenomenon depicted above?
- Which one of the following, if true, most helps to resolve the above paradox?

For explanation questions, note that you will be asked to resolve a set of statements that seem to contradict each other. A paradox is a proposal that seems self-contradictory or absurd at first, but after close inspection, it actually resolves the issue or is proven to be true. Let's look at an example of a paradox question below:

> At the turn of the twenty-first century, Portugal reformed many of its drug use policies, including decriminalization of drugs and social policy changes centered on health. In 2014, there were only fifteen drug-related deaths in Portugal compared to 112 in 2000.

Which one of the following, if true, most helps to resolve the apparent paradox?

We are looking for an answer explanation that will solve the paradox of this statement. Typically, we would expect drug use and drug-related deaths to skyrocket if people were not being punished for drug use. However, this is not the case. The following might be a valid reason why the opposite of what we expected to happen has happened:

People in possession of drugs are now being sent to treatment facilities instead of prison; treatment facilities have higher success rates in preventing relapse and empowering addicts to stop drug use opposed to punitive measures used inside prisons.

The explanation above helps to explain the paradox of the lowering of drug-related deaths. Social policy changes as well as decriminalization have both had a hand in the reduction of deaths. Some answer choices might try to throw you off by talking about deaths in other countries, or may throw in an answer choice meant to confuse the reality of the stem. Don't fall for these. What's stated in the question stem is the end-all. You are simply looking for the most reasonable explanation that resolves the paradox within the statements.

Practice Questions

For the questions below, choose the best answer that completes the question. Some of the answers may be close to the correct answer; however, you are to choose the answer choice that best answers the question.

1. Analyst: The Mars teams "X" and "Z" recently began working on simulations that would prepare them to live on the red planet in approximately twenty years. The leader of team "X," Brittany, recently requested more team members, due to the number of discrepancies she found in the technological sector. Even now, team "X" continues to find twice the number of discrepancies in their technological sector than team "Z." Therefore, we can assume that team "X" is doing a very poor job compared to team "Z."

Which of the following, if true, most seriously weakens the analyst's argument?
   a. Team "Z" will go to Mars five years sooner than team "X" if they avoid excessive errors and pass all their safety tests in time.
   b. Since team "X" hired more team members for the technological sector, the biological sector has had to get rid of two of their own members.
   c. Team "Z" spends 30 percent of their hours checking for discrepancies, while team "X" spends 10 percent of their hours checking for discrepancies.
   d. Team "Z" gets paid much higher than its competitor, team "X."
   e. Team "X" spends 25 percent of their hours checking for discrepancies, while team "Z" spends 5 percent of their hours checking for discrepancies.

2. The opioid epidemic is running rampant throughout the United States. Pharmaceutical players such as Johnson and Johnson, Purdue Pharma, and Teva Pharmaceuticals have done little for the health of the nation. Ironically, they've made the nation's population sicker than ever. In order to curb the nation's drug epidemic, lawmakers must impose stricter regulations on the distribution and prescription of these substances.

This argument requires assuming which one of the following principles?
   a. The pharmaceutical industry is responsible for the nation's opioid epidemic and should pay for the recovery and wellness of those harmed due to their negligence.
   b. Creating harsher punishments for people who abuse substances is an unavoidable step in the process to treat substance use disorder.
   c. The abuse of substances in the U.S. is proportional to the amount and ease of substances that are available to be used.
   d. The United States is leading in terms of drug addiction and has the most deaths per year due to opioids compared to any other country.
   e. Lawmakers are the only ones who can turn the drug epidemic around by imposing stricter laws on everyone involved.

3. There are many misconceptions about a writer's process. Many believe a writer's process involves a great deal of inspiration. However, a writer's process has less to do with inspiration and more to do with discipline. The habit of showing up to the paper and writing things down every single day is a surer way of becoming a writer than relying on the fickle movement of inspiration.

Which of the following arguments is most similar in its reasoning to the argument above?

a. Many people believe that athleticism is genetic and that people are "born to be great" in whatever sport they participate in. However, someone's athletic ability has more to do with practice than with innate athleticism. Going to practice every single day for years and years is what enables athletes to succeed.

b. Everyone agrees that one of the most important skills that a painter must have is a "good eye." Having a "good eye" means being able to determine a subject and assessing its potential to be recreated in art. Someone who is born without a "good eye" will not have much success in the painting world.

c. Writers are people who want to understand the world more. Through writing, they are able to make sense of the great mysteries of life, such as death and love. Their audience is important for feedback, and so that the writers can have the purpose of inviting someone else in on their journey of discovery.

d. The process of becoming a photographer is very difficult. First, one must know what kind of pictures he or she will want to take so that the right kind of camera for specific environments can be purchased. Additionally, one must have the means to pay for a quality camera and its equipment. There are many steps to take in honing one's photography skill, but the results might be worth it.

e. Bull riding is one of the world's most dangerous sports. A flank strap is used on the bull to cause the animal to buck, thus making it harder for the bull rider to stay on. Additionally, when the bull rider is thrown off of the bull, he or she must avoid being gored by the horns.

4. A study done in 1992 delved into what would be negative effects of the drug PMR, which had just come onto the market that same year, and was used for maintaining blood pressure. Among the effects were swelling of the abdomen, skin disintegration, and complications during childbirth. Because of these disastrous findings, the drug was discontinued in 1993. Another study done in 1994 was concerned to see that complications during childbirth were up 30 percent in the year 1992; 1991 and 1993 had similar results pertaining to childbirth complications. From these findings, we can assume that the first study was correct; the negative effects of the drug PMR included complications during childbirth as one of its most catastrophic effects.

The reasoning in the argument is most vulnerable to criticism on the grounds that the argument

a. makes a circular reasoning based on the results.

b. mistakes correlation for causation.

c. erroneously provides the opposite of the wrong answer to be true.

d. uses a red herring to distract from the argument's purpose.

e. attacks the source of the argument.

5. Brazil nuts are a food source high in selenium, which is known for its anti-inflammatory properties. Inflammation is known to be at the source of diseases such as cancer and high blood pressure, so consuming anti-inflammatory foods would help to avoid cancer and disease. Therefore, everyone who eats brazil nuts will avoid cancer.

The pattern of flawed reasoning in which one of the following arguments is most parallel to that in the argument above?

    a. Cashews are a food source high in magnesium. Magnesium is extremely important for heart health, increasing energy, and preventing migraines. Cashews also contain Iron, which transports oxygen throughout the body.

    b. Brown rice is a food that is known to contain arsenic, which can harm the human body. Arsenic is known to play a role in the development of cancer and diabetes, so consuming arsenic would potentially cause someone to become sick. Therefore, everyone who eats brown rice will become sick.

    c. Oranges do not contain Vitamin D. Those looking to add Vitamin D to their diets should incorporate tofu, shiitake mushrooms, or spinach. Vitamin D is important for calcium absorption and bone growth. Vitamin D deficiency is often linked to certain types of cancer and weight gain.

    d. Whales have lungs instead of gills. Whales are mammals, and therefore use lungs to breathe when they come up to the surface of the water. When whales go beneath the water, they simply hold their breath until it is time to come up again. Everyone should know about whales because they are interesting creatures.

    e. Microwaves contain high levels of RF radiation in order to warm up foods. Exposure to radiation can lead to radiation poisoning, which can cause symptoms such as vomiting, headaches, and fatigue. Therefore, some people who own microwaves may experience flu-like symptoms if exposed to too much radiation.

6. Jackson: In his new collection, Merwin has been working on translating Spanish poems into English. His translations are less focused on the accuracy of the language and more on creating a similar work of art in English as in Spanish. He attempts to alter the literal meaning of the words to retain the beauty of the original text. This is a new, yet improved, method of translation work, as some translations I've read have been unfortunate rewrites of wonderful works of art in their original language.

Hardy: However, the refusal to adhere to a literal translation could create many problems for the original text. The beauty of the text has as much to do with the intended meaning of the work than with the attraction of the language. This is an adaptation in modern translation that will cause the true meaning of the original text to be lost on its foreign readers.

Which one of the following most accurately expresses a point of disagreement between Jackson and Hardy?

    a. Whether modern translation can be used in a pedagogy to offer students a more interesting viewpoint compared to traditional translation.

    b. Whether translating Spanish into English is a worthwhile pursuit, given that a rendering from one language to the next would most certainly result in the Spanish language being lost in translation.

    c. Whether English is attractive enough a language to be used for translation work and what to do about the future of English translation in the future.

    d. Whether or not modern translation adheres to the beauty of the original text by avoiding a literal rendering of that text.

    e. Whether the purpose of translation work is honoring the original author or honoring the translator, and what the ethical implications of comparing the two are.

7. Critical theory teacher: Heidegger's summation of language is far too ceremonial to be taken seriously. He states that "language speaks man," an idea that man could not exist without language, rather than language not existing without man. Language is about play, and the theory of it should not be taken so seriously. Therefore, we are going to focus more on Baudrillard's philosophy of thought, which includes the treatment of popular culture and its erasure of "the real" in its attempt to make technology itself "more real" than reality.

Which one of the following is an assumption the critical theory teacher's argument requires?
    a. The examination of popular culture related to theory and its treatment of technology as a replacement for reality is lighthearted enough to focus on in the critical theory teacher's class.
    b. Critical theory classes should only teach topics which are fun and lighthearted. In this way, students will be more receptive to theory, which is usually seen as unbearably complex and boring.
    c. Heidegger's summation of language, although ceremonial, is at least as important as Baudrillard's examination of popular culture and technology.
    d. There are not enough university classes that offer a lighthearted perspective of critical theory; most of them focus on the most complex aspects of theory and skip the playful side of it.
    e. Students who study Heidegger's philosophy of thought relating to the placement of language in existence are no better than students who study Baudrillard's philosophy of thought relating to pop culture and technology.

8. Professor: I have two students who are equally talented in the work that they do. The first one is a writer and the second one is a cartoonist. I have to choose one to give an award of talent to. Both writers and cartoonists are equally recognized in the work they produce, so I can't choose one based on exposure. One student, the cartoonist, gives twenty percent more effort than the writer does, although they both give a good amount of effort to the coursework. However, I think since the cartoonist gives that extra push of performance to their talent, I will be choosing them for the talent award.

Which one of the following principles, if valid, most helps to justify the professor's reasoning?
    a. It is better to gift a single award to a person who puts in more effort than a person who has the same amount of talent who puts in less effort.
    b. If two people are equally talented and their work had equal exposure, yet one worked harder than the other, the harder worker would be considered the better person.
    c. If two people's occupation have the same amount of exposure, then their skill level should be assessed by measuring the amount of effort they put into their projects.
    d. It is better to give awards to people who put in more effort than people who have the same amount of talent who puts in less effort, as long as their chosen occupations have similar exposure.
    e. It is better to gift a single award to a person who puts in more effort than a person who has the same amount of talent who puts in less effort, as long as their chosen occupations have similar exposure.

9. For the purpose of increasing sales, Green Eats Café added a parking lot in the empty space behind their building in addition to their street parking out front. However, the café's sales decreased after the parking lot was added in the empty space in the back of the building.

Which one of the following, if true, most helps to explain the decrease in sales?
    a. Most people who go to Green Eats Café live downtown and therefore walk to the café rather than use any kind of transportation.
    b. Green Eats Café was forced to add parking meters in their new parking lot after they built it.
    c. The two stores on either side of Green Eats started renovations after the parking lot was added and the construction has deterred customers from visiting the café.
    d. Very soon after the new parking lot was added, the city added new stoplights on the street the café is on.
    e. A few weeks before the parking lot was built, there was a huge storm that caused flooding to all the stores on that street, including Green Eats Café.

10. With the new Chaucer Café for Cats, most of the town's stray cat problem has been solved. After all, the café not only serves premium coffee and baked goods, but _____.

The conclusion of the argument is most strongly supported if which one of the following completes the passage?
    a. provides a safe space, food, and vaccinations for 75 percent of the town's stray cats and has open adoption auctions while customers drink their coffee.
    b. cares for and allows cats that are up for adoption to roam around while customers are enjoying their morning coffee.
    c. when customers go to pay for their coffee or baked goods, there is a donation jar at the register to encourage donations to the stray cat shelter down the street.
    d. has done everything in its power to solve the stray cat problem while also serving coffee and baked goods to its customers.
    e. the stray cat problem will continue to happen if Chaucer Café for Cats doesn't keep doing what they're doing in order to stop the problem.

11. Publisher: Although the average American is reading more books than ever before, they're increasingly reading books on their phones, tablets, and computers. Consequently, brick-and-mortar bookstores are in rapid decline. As a result, publishers need to focus more on the design and interface of digital editions to remain commercially viable.

Which one of the following most accurately expresses the publisher's main conclusion?
    a. Publishers can't survive without brick-and-mortar stores.
    b. There's room for improvement in digital editions.
    c. The transition from paper to electronic books is disrupting the publishing industry
    d. Publishers must adapt to the increasing demand for digital editions.
    e. Digital editions are more profitable per copy than paper editions.

12. All of the school's senior high school students passed their literature, math, and science state exams this year. The student's test scores ranged from 70% to 100%, and on average, the students performed the best on the science exam. Passing all of the state exams is a graduation requirement. Thus, all of the school's seniors will graduate this year.

Which one of the following is an assumption required by the argument?
   a. The minimum score to pass a state exam is 70%.
   b. The science exam is the most important state exam.
   c. Literature, math, and science are the only state exams.
   d. There are additional graduation requirements.
   e. No junior high school student is graduating a year early.

13. Economist: The country's economy has faced numerous obstacles over the past decade, resulting in a prolonged recession. For example, automation and outsourcing have wreaked havoc in the country's job market. In response, the government enacted bipartisan economic reform that drove unemployment down to an all-time low. As a result, the country's economy has fully recovered.

The economist's argument most strongly supports which one of the following statements?
   a. Outsourcing was the primary cause of the country's prolonged recession.
   b. High unemployment can threaten a country's economic health.
   c. Bipartisan economic policies are always the most effective.
   d. Automation and outsourcing continue to challenge the country's economy.
   e. Unemployment needed to reach an all-time low before the country's economy recovered.

14. Salesman: After hitting my commission cap last week, I won't be earning any money on my sales for the rest of this financial quarter. I'm essentially working for free, and I might as well just watch videos on my computer all day. This is clearly a detriment to our company's future growth.

Manager: You're also being paid a base salary. That's enough incentive to work hard for our other employees who don't receive a commission. If you watch videos on your computer all day, or otherwise waste the company's time, you'll be fired.

Which one of the following best describes the main issue in dispute between the salesman and manager?
   a. An employee who watches videos at work is a detriment to their company.
   b. The salesman deserves a special status in the company.
   c. A commission cap undermines the salesman's incentive to work.
   d. The company would suffer if employees don't work hard.
   e. Employees shouldn't have to work for free.

15. Policymaker: Drugs ruin people's lives. I know more than a dozen people who lost their jobs over drugs. And that's to say nothing about the impact on their families. The Drug Enforcement Agency has recently called for aggressive action to restrict the availability of drugs in our country. Thus, we must criminalize all drugs.

Which one of the following reasoning errors most weakens the policymaker's argument?
   a. The policymaker relies on a hasty generalization.
   b. The policymaker appeals to an inappropriate authority.
   c. The policymaker fails to resolve a conflict of interest in his cited authority.
   d. The policymaker mistakes a probability for a certainty.
   e. The policymaker fails to define an important term in his argument, causing confusion.

16. Ethicist: The overarching goal for human civilization should be to reduce the suffering of conscious beings to zero. Animals are conscious beings; thus, the human species should universally adopt vegetarianism. However, dietary problems and prohibitive costs prevent some people from transitioning to vegetarianism. In the near future, lab-grown meat will enter the market and overcome those barriers, thereby achieving our goal.

Which one of the following, if true, most strengthens the ethicist's argument?
    a. Lab-grown meat is more environmentally sustainable than animal flesh.
    b. No animals suffer during the creation of lab-grown meat.
    c. Some people eat animal flesh strictly based on its superior taste.
    d. Lab-grown meat is half the cost of animal flesh.
    e. Compared to animal flesh, lab-grown meat's quality control will be easier to regulate.

17. A company specializes in designing and manufacturing women's coats. After many successful years, the company's sales have plummeted, including a record low last year. Industry insiders have speculated that the company's switch to a cheaper material has caused the precipitous drop in sales. Nevertheless, the company earned record-high profits last year.

Which one of the following, if true, best resolves the apparent paradox?
    a. The company started licensing its designs last year for the first time.
    b. The cheaper material allows the company to charge less per coat at retail.
    c. The company hired marketing and sales consultants last year.
    d. Many coat manufacturers have also experienced a dramatic decline in sales.
    e. The cheaper material is indistinguishable from what the company previously used.

18. The Knights are the best baseball team because no other baseball team is as good as them. Barry Jones, a professional baseball talent scout, believes the Knights' offense is so powerful that they will be able to score at least ten runs again anyone. No other team has scored ten runs in a game, so the Knights seem like a strong contender to win the championship.

Which one of the following most accurately states a flaw in the argument's reasoning?
    a. The argument appeals to an improper authority.
    b. The argument engages in circular reasoning.
    c. The argument includes an ad hominem argument.
    d. The argument's internal logic is self-contradictory.
    e. The argument relies on an emotional appeal.

19. Xavier: Our society's consumption is immoral. We're all constantly consuming items produced overseas in countries with no labor protection. The workers who produced every piece of clothing we're currently wearing earned less than a dollar for their day's labor. Even worse, we only use these products for a short period, ensuring that the demand for cheap products remains artificially high, which is environmentally unsustainable.

Willie: The standard of living in those countries is much lower than in our own. Although the workers' compensation might seem unfair, the dollar has significantly more buying power in the countries in question. Those workers can buy three meals every day, afford rent, and save for the future. Before the factories arrived, their only option was subsistence agriculture. If anything, our consumption of cheaply manufactured goods is highly moral. Increased manufacturing is part of the industrialization process, like what our country went through centuries ago. As long as manufacturing continues, these countries will continue developing, thereby raising the population's standard of living.

Willie responds to Xavier's argument by:
    a. rejecting the place of morality in a discussion of economics.
    b. addressing the problem of using products for short periods of time.
    c. describing how industrialization is different in every country.
    d. defending cheap manufacturing solely based on differences in buying power.
    e. reframing the foreign workers' compensation with additional context.

20. Brian shared his lunch with his classmate, Janet, when she forgot her lunch at home. But when Brian forgot his lunch, he didn't expect Janet to share her lunch with him. Thus, Brian is a moral person.

Which one of the following most closely conforms to the principle illustrated by the argument above?
    a. Christina shared her candy with her classmate Chelsea, but Chelsea didn't share her candy with Christina. Thus, Christina is a moral person.
    b. Abraham is a moral person. While visiting a friend in a foreign country, Abraham paid for a random stranger's dinner.
    c. Joseph is a moral person. Joseph loaned his friend money to buy a car, and his friend never paid him back.
    d. Tanya offered to drive her coworker home after her car broke down. Thus, Tanya is a moral person.
    e. Holden shared his lunch with his classmate Olivia, and when Holden forget his lunch, Olivia didn't share it with him. Thus, Holden is a moral person.

21. All dogs have tails, and all cats have tails. So, dogs and cats are similar.

Which one of the following most closely parallels the argument?
    a. Dogs and cats share one similarity, so they're the same.
    b. High school teachers and professors both work with students.
    c. Some dogs are black, and all cats are black. So, dogs and cats are similar.
    d. Computers and sweatshirts are similar. All computers are made in China, and all sweatshirts are made in China.
    e. All lawyers are liars, and George is a liar; therefore, George must be a lawyer.

22. Most conservatives oppose a large government. If someone opposes large government, then they must favor tax cuts, and all people who favor tax cuts are moral. All people over the age of sixty are conservatives, except those who hold college degrees. Jim opposes a large government.

Assuming the statements above are correct, which one of the following must be true?
- a. Jim is a conservative.
- b. Jim doesn't favor tax cuts.
- c. Jim is over the age of sixty.
- d. Jim holds a college degree.
- e. Jim is moral.

23. Scientist: There's a growing movement against vaccination. These people argue that vaccines cause illness, but nothing could be further from the truth. Vaccines have played a critical role in fighting deadly infectious diseases, like smallpox, polio, and mumps. In addition, numerous government agencies license and regulate these vaccines to ensure they're safe for public consumption. There's no empirical support that links any vaccine with causing any disease. If people stop taking vaccines, a public health crisis will be inevitable. Politicians must make a more concerted effort, as well as invest more money, to educate the public about vaccines.

The scientist's argument proceeds by:
- a. stating a conclusion that's followed by a series of supporting statements.
- b. listing illustrative examples.
- c. identifying an issue and describing why that issue poses a limited risk.
- d. debunking an opposing view and concluding with a policy proposal.
- e. developing a hypothesis to explain the cause of a new phenomenon.

24. Monetization on the Internet depends exclusively on exposure. Companies seek to gain exposure through search engine optimization and advertisements. Advertisements are the most effective for new products, while search engine optimization works well only for companies with a lot of preexisting content. A new Internet-based golf supply company is launching their first line of golf clubs.

Which one of the following conclusions most logically follows from the argument?
- a. The company should gain exposure before launching the product.
- b. The company should invest in advertisements.
- c. The company should invest in search engine optimization.
- d. The company should combine advertisements and search engine optimization.
- e. The company should gain exposure through a viral marketing strategy.

25. Male Technician: Computing power is advancing exponentially. Today, my current cell phone has more than one hundred times the computing power than the first cell phone I bought ten years ago. However, my current cell phone's battery dies faster than any cell phone I've ever owned. Cell phone companies need to create batteries that can accommodate increased computing power.

Which one of the following assumptions does the technician's argument rely upon most?
- a. Increased computing power strains cell phone batteries.
- b. The technician's current cell phone is defective.
- c. The technician's first cell phone was already outdated when it was purchased.
- d. Computing power will continue to increase in the foreseeable future.
- e. Increased computing power improves cell phones.

26. Jalen: Football will be extinct in less than twenty years. Modern-day football players are simply too big and too fast, and when they collide, traumatic brain injury is inevitable. Even repetitive minor collisions can cause long-term injury. Collisions can't be removed from the game without killing the product.

Liz: Traumatic brain injury does pose a threat to football, but your assessment is overly pessimistic. There are many opportunities for reform. Weight limits could be established. More rigorous testing of performance enhancing drugs could be implemented. Dangerous collisions could be more heavily punished. You're right that minor collisions can't be avoided without ruining football, but players are assuming that risk by playing an inherently dangerous game.

The dialogue provides the most support for the claim that Jalen and Liz disagree over whether:
    a. current football players are too big and too fast.
    b. current football players are risking traumatic brain injury.
    c. minor collisions can still cause brain injury.
    d. football is inherently dangerous.
    e. some degree of risk is acceptable.

27. Law School Student: It's unreasonable to give law school students closed-book tests that require memorization. Nobody would expect a lawyer to know the answer to all their client's questions off the top of their head. Research is an essential part of being a lawyer. Closed-book tests are especially unfair in Professor Lockhart's evidence class due to the number of rules he requires his students to know.

Which one of the following most accurately states why the law school student's argument is vulnerable to criticism?
    a. The student draws a faulty analogy.
    b. The student begs the question.
    c. The student introduces a red herring.
    d. The student mistakes cause and effect.
    e. The student attacks a person's character.

28. Janet is an outstanding student who is looking to pursue higher education. She will graduate as the valedictorian of the country's top academic high school, and she achieved a perfect score on the entrance exam for college. In addition, Janet volunteers every weekend at a soup kitchen. High school grades and entrance exam performances are the only merit-based criteria, and college admission is exclusively merit-based.

Which one of the following most logically completes the argument?
    a. Janet will be the most intelligent senior that graduates high school this year.
    b. Janet's volunteer work will strengthen her college applications.
    c. Janet will only apply to the best academic colleges in the country.
    d. Janet will likely write the best personal statement to accompany her college applications.
    e. Janet will likely be accepted into every college that she applies to.

29. Alexandra: Participation trophies embody everything that's wrong with our society. Competition is intended to teach children how to work hard and strive for success. As such, participation trophies should be banned since they send the wrong message. Yeah, sometimes there will be disappointment, but that's life. If everyone is a winner, then nobody is a winner.

Zachary: You're mischaracterizing the situation. Participation trophies haven't replaced all other trophies. Individual and/or team success is almost always rewarded with a superior trophy, and the rest of the children usually receive participation trophies. Children naturally gravitate toward what's special, and they'll work harder the next time to win the superior trophy. But in the meantime, the participation trophies recognize their efforts and incentivize future attempts.

Alexandra and Zachary would most likely agree on which one of the following?
    a. Future participation should be incentivized.
    b. Receiving a participation trophy is a major disappointment.
    c. Encouraging children to work hard is important.
    d. Competition should reflect life.
    e. Life is full of disappointments.

30. Criminologist: Every jurisdiction should legalize the death penalty. The purpose of punishment is to deter people from committing crimes, and there's no greater deterrent than death. The resulting reduction in crime would outweigh all of the death penalty's costs.

Which one of the following, if true, most weakens the criminologist's argument?
    a. Some innocent people would be executed.
    b. All criminals can be rehabilitated.
    c. Most criminals aren't rational actors.
    d. Executions cost the state more money and resources than life sentences.
    e. Public opinion overwhelmingly opposes the death penalty.

31. The best breakfast beverage is the one in which the amount of caffeine can be customized in every cup. Both tea and coffee contain caffeine. However, tea is limited to what's in the bag, and every cup of coffee from a pot or machine has the same dose of caffeine. In contrast, instant coffee's dose of caffeine can be customized based on the amount of powder that's added to the cup; thus, instant coffee is the best breakfast beverage.

Which one of the following, if true, would weaken the argument?
    a. Tea is the best tasting breakfast beverage.
    b. Instant coffee tastes terrible.
    c. Tea bags can be combined.
    d. Espresso has more caffeine than coffee.
    e. Excessive consumption of caffeine is unhealthy.

32. Thomas is either a fireman or a policeman. Thomas is not a fireman; thus, he is a policeman.

Which one of the following most closely parallels the argument's reasoning?
    a. Cats can only be white or black. The cat is not white, so the cat must be black.
    b. Lisa will be promoted to either CEO or CFO when she graduates from business school.
    c. Tate is a mailman. If he weren't a mailman, Tate would want to be a dog walker.
    d. All super villains have a lair. Chris is a super villain; thus, Chris has a lair.
    e. Holly either works in HR, sales, or accounting. Holly doesn't work in HR; thus, she works in either sales or accounting.

33. Director: Movies require the audience to suspend their disbelief. As such, directors need to create a universe with consistent internal logic. When the subject matter is based on real events and communities, the director must closely mirror reality. For example, characters should talk like people from that specific region and historical period.

Critic: Movies hold immense power in our culture in defining what is and isn't socially acceptable. Consequently, directors have a responsibility not to use language that offends various groups, especially people in vulnerable positions. Censoring hate speech and racial slurs won't break the audience's disbelief.

Which one of the following best describes the main point in dispute between the director and critic?
    a. Movie audiences suspend their disbelief.
    b. Hate speech and racial slurs offend people.
    c. Movies should avoid offending people.
    d. Directors enjoy full creative control over their work.
    e. Movies have enormous cultural relevancy.

34. Christina's chair has a squeaky wheel. When her coworker Andrew went to the bathroom, Christina switched their chairs. Christina is justified, because last week Andrew switched chairs with Felix without asking him.

Which one of the following most closely conforms to the principle illustrated by the argument above?
    a. Tyler cheated on his taxes because the government uses its revenue to fund immoral initiatives.
    b. Diana stole a loaf of bread because the store overcharged her for eggs.
    c. Mary switched seats with Abe when Abe went to the bathroom.
    d. Phillip stole Jackie's book. Jackie had originally stolen the same book from Igor.
    e. Tanya ate Samantha's sandwich. Samantha's mom makes her lunch every day.

35. Economist: The modern economy is increasingly dependent on the Internet. This year, for the first time in history, online retailers will surpass physical stores in total sales. The Internet eliminates middlemen, decreasing the prices for consumers, and entrepreneurs can raise funds quickly on the Internet, lowering the barrier for entry into markets. Many people also participate in the gig economy to earn extra money. However, new proposed regulations threaten to undermine the Internet's growth. If these regulations pass. . .

Which one of the following best completes the economist's argument?
    a. the economy will spiral into a depression.
    b. the economy will suffer a major setback.
    c. physical stores will dominate online retailers.
    d. entrepreneurship will decline.
    e. the gig economy will collapse.

36. High school students need to take an entrance exam before applying to college. The exam tests students' language and math skills. While high school grades and extracurricular activities are important, the results of this exam will largely determine where students are accepted into college. Ms. Wilson teaches an exam preparation class, and she thinks there's a high likelihood of all her current students passing the exam. Molly is a current student, and she recently sat for the exam; therefore, Molly will be accepted into college.

Which one of the following is a flaw in the argument's reasoning?
    a. The argument mistakes a necessary and sufficient condition.
    b. The argument uses the same term in different ways.
    c. The argument fails to define an important term.
    d. The argument appeals to an inappropriate authority.
    e. The argument makes a hasty generalization.

37. Historian: The United States dropped atomic bombs on Hiroshima and Nagasaki at the end of World War II. The two bombs killed more than one hundred thousand Japanese civilians. Prior to the bombings, Japan refused to surrender despite the tides of war decisively turning against them. If not for the use of atomic weapons, an estimated two hundred thousand Americans would've died during the invasion, and Japan might have suffered as many as one million civilian casualties. In addition, Japanese troops committed unthinkable war crimes throughout the war, killing more than ten million civilians.

Which one of the following best describes the conclusion set forth by the historian?
    a. Japan deserved to be bombed with nuclear weapons.
    b. Japan forced the United States to use nuclear weapons.
    c. The decision to use nuclear weapons was easy.
    d. Nuclear weapons were the least bad option available.
    e. Japan couldn't have won World War II.

38. Trainer: Heart disease is the leading cause of death in this country. Cardio and weightlifting help the heart in two ways. First, they burn calories and create the caloric deficit necessary to sustain weight loss. Second, they decrease resting heart rate by increasing blood flow in every heartbeat, so fewer beats are required.

Nutritionist: Exercise must be accompanied by a healthy diet to effectively prevent heart disease. The body requires a protein-rich diet to gain muscle, and no amount of exercise can achieve a caloric deficit with an unhealthy diet. Consequently, a healthy diet is the foundation for weight loss.

The trainer and nutritionist would most agree on which one of the following?
    a. Weight loss is more important than building muscle.
    b. Exercise should be accompanied with a healthy diet.
    c. A caloric deficit can decrease an individual's resting heart rate.
    d. The amount of exercise and diet differs from person to person.
    e. Some people would benefit from losing weight.

39. Over the last two decades the world has achieved a new record for global food production every single year. However, an unprecedented number of people died from starvation due to food shortage last year.

Which one of the following best resolves the apparent paradox?
    a. The increase in food production is mostly limited to simple carbohydrates.
    b. Subsistence agriculture has become practically nonexistent.
    c. Corporate farms are dominating the agricultural industry at the expense of family farms.
    d. Income inequality also hit an all-time high last year.
    e. The rate of population growth exceeds the annual increase in food production.

40. Ethicist: Artificial intelligence is rapidly approaching consciousness. What began as simple algorithms that locate and regurgitate information is now capable of independently drawing conclusions. Unfortunately, the free market is responsible for the advances in artificial intelligence, and private companies aren't incentivized to align artificial intelligence with humanity's goals. Without any guidance, artificial intelligence will adopt humanity's worst impulses and mirror the Internet's most violent worldviews.

The ethicist would most likely agree with which one of the following?
    a. The Internet is negatively impacting society.
    b. Unregulated artificial intelligence is a threat to humanity.
    c. Humanity's goals should always be prioritized over technological advancements.
    d. Artificial intelligence should be limited to simple algorithms.
    e. All conscious beings, including those with artificial intelligence, are owed civil rights.

41. A shadow government is running our country. Their goal is to increase weapons sales by inciting a global conflict. A government spokesman recently rejected the existence of a shadow government, but the spokesman is a known adulterer. If he can't be faithful to his wife, there's no way he would protect the public's interest against the shadow government.

The argument is most vulnerable to criticism on the grounds that it:
    a. argues from authority.
    b. relies on an emotional appeal.
    c. makes an ad hominem attack.
    d. introduces a red herring.
    e. insists on a slippery slope.

42. Psychologist: Children who play video games are more likely to act more aggressively when interacting with their peers. Video games with graphic depictions of gun violence are the most dangerous to children's cognitive development. The problem is becoming more pronounced as children start to receive cell phones at younger ages. Without an intervention by the government, this country's violent crime rate is going to skyrocket.

The strength of the psychologist's argument depends on which one of the following?
    a. Violent video games weren't popular ten years ago.
    b. Children don't naturally play aggressively.
    c. The government is legally obligated to prevent violent crimes.
    d. Children have access to guns.
    e. Video games can be played on cell phones.

43. If the government invests in alternative energy sources, then the threat of climate change will be mitigated. If the government fails to make an investment, then the country will go bankrupt due to extreme weather events. A bankrupt government will not be able to fund its military. The government will only invest in alternative energy sources when the Green Party controls 51 seats in the legislature. During this legislative session, the Green Party controls 22 seats, but 60 Green Party politicians are projected to win seats in the upcoming election.

According to the passage above, what must follow?
    a. The financial cost per extreme weather events will increase during this legislative session.
    b. The country won't be able to fund its military during this legislative session.
    c. The government will invest in alternative energy sources during the next legislative session.
    d. The threat of climate change will be mitigated during this legislative session.
    e. Voters support making an investment in alternative energy sources.

44. Online colleges are superior to the in-person experience. The world's best colleges now offer courses online. Tuition at online colleges is significantly less, and they typically use course material that's freely available online. Coursework can also be completed at the student's own pace, providing students with greater flexibility. As a result, it's much easier for students pursuing an online degree to work full-time.

Each of the following, if true, would weaken the argument EXCEPT:
    a. The primary benefit to attending a physical college is the networking events held on campus.
    b. Online college students don't have the same structural support and resources.
    c. None of the best colleges offer enough courses to earn a degree from one of those colleges.
    d. Students pursuing online degrees don't need to commute.
    e. Employers consistently underestimate the value of online college degrees.

45. All wealthy people have worked hard, except those born into wealthy families. No wealthy person owns less than two homes. Some poor people work harder than any wealthy person and still can't afford rent. Jonathan is a wealthy person.

Which one of the following must be true?
    a. Jonathan has worked hard.
    b. Jonathan was born into a wealthy family.
    c. Jonathan was poor growing up.
    d. Jonathan owns at least two homes.
    e. Jonathan can't afford rent.

46. Businessman: My cardinal rule is to only invest in privately-held small businesses that exclusively sell tangible goods and have no debt.

Which one of the following is the best investment opportunity according to the businessman's cardinal rule?
    a. Jose owns his own grocery store. He's looking for a partner, because he fell behind on his mortgage and owes the bank three months' worth of payments.
    b. Elizabeth is seeking a partner with business expertise to help expand her standalone store that sells niche board games. The store isn't currently profitable, but it's never been in debt.
    c. A family-owned accounting firm with no outstanding debts is looking for its first outside investor. The firm has turned a profit every year since it opened
    d. A multinational corporation is selling high-yield bonds for the first time.
    e. A regional chain of liquor stores is selling the licensing rights for a new franchise to help repay its initial small business loan.

47. Journalist: Our newspaper should only consider the truth in its reporting. When a party is clearly in the wrong, like if he or she is spreading a pernicious false narrative, their position should never be presented alongside the truth without comment. The purpose of journalism is to deliver facts and context. Both sides of an issue should be called for comment, but their responses should be framed appropriately, especially when there's a potential conflict of interest or source of bias at play. Our editorial board needs to seriously consider how our newspaper isn't currently meeting these basic standards, exposing us to charges of bias from all sides.

Which one of the following most accurately identifies the primary purpose of the journalist's argument?
    a. Persuade the newspaper to adopt a more rigorous approach to journalism.
    b. Defend the newspaper against charges of bias in its reporting.
    c. Argue for the newspaper to hire more journalists with the appropriate skills.
    d. Define the professional responsibilities of a journalist.
    e. Explain the newspaper's editorial standards.

48. Ecologist: If we do not act now, more than one hundred animal species will be extinct by the end of the decade. The best way to save them is to sell hunting licenses for endangered species. Hunters can pay for the right to kill old and lame animals. Otherwise, there's no way to fund our conservation efforts.

Which one of the following assumptions does the ecologist's argument rely upon?
    a. Hunting licenses for non-endangered species aren't profitable.
    b. All one hundred animal species must be saved.
    c. The new hunting license revenue will fund conservation efforts.
    d. Conservation efforts should've began last decade.
    e. It is physically impossible for old and lame animals to reproduce.

49. Politician: Every cigarette smoked cost the city more than $1,000. Smokers are bankrupting our healthcare system. Discarded filters pollute our waterways, and second-hand smoke poisons our airways, threatening all pedestrians. The city must ban tobacco smoking immediately.

Which one of the following, if true, would most strengthen the politician's argument?
    a. Placing a high tax on tobacco hasn't reduced smoking at all.
    b. Smoking cigarettes is already banned in bars and restaurants.
    c. The city's waterways and airways also suffer from heavy industrial pollution.
    d. Many tobacco substitutes are readily available.
    e. The state government is also considering a ban on tobacco.

50. Today is Monday. If John is on the red line, he's visiting his doctor. Whenever John visits his doctor, he treats himself to ice cream on his way home. If John is on the green line, he's visiting his lawyer. John never visits his lawyer on a Monday.

Which one of the following must be true?
    a. John will visit his doctor on Monday.
    b. John will not visit his doctor on Monday.
    c. John will treat himself to ice cream on Monday.
    d. John will take the red line on Monday.
    e. John will not take the green line on Monday.

Answer Explanations

1. E: Choice *E* is the best answer choice here. It says "Team 'X' spends 25 percent of their hours checking for discrepancies, while team 'Z' spends 5 percent of their hours checking for discrepancies." This answer choice would most seriously weaken the analyst's argument that team "X" is doing a poor job compared to team "Z." We see with the new information that the issue *is* being corrected. If team "X" spends 25 percent of their hours checking for issues, and team "Z" only spends 5 percent, then not only will team "X" find more issues, but they will be able to fix these issues. Team "Z" may have as many issues as team "X" does, but they have less hours dedicated to checking these issues. We can see that team "X" has more issues because they check more, not because they are doing a poor job.

Choice *A* is incorrect. The fact that team "Z" would go to Mars five years sooner does not weaken the analyst's argument that team "Z" is doing a better job than team "X," because the choice is conditional on "Z" avoiding excessive errors and passing all their safety tests, and has nothing to do with team "X."

Choice *B* is incorrect. This answer states that "since team "X" hired more team members for the technological sector, the biological sector has had to get rid of two of their own members." Although this is unfortunate, it does not weaken the argument that team "X" is doing a poor job compared to team "Z." This only gives one of the results of the discrepancies found.

Choice *C* is incorrect because this would strengthen the analyst's argument. Team "X" would indeed be doing a poor job if they spent only 10 percent of their time checking for discrepancies rather than 30 percent, but yet find twice the number of errors.

Choice *D* is really irrelevant to the question. It may be tempting to base team "X's" success on their pay, and this choice may be a factor in a deciding vote, but this is not the *best* answer choice available.

2. C: Choice *C* is the best answer here. The argument is that "in order to curb the drug epidemic, lawmakers must impose stricter regulations on the distribution and prescription of these substances." The argument assumes that the availability of substances corresponds to people's abuse of them. Therefore, the argument contends that a decrease in availability of these drugs will cause substance abuse to subside.

Choice *A* is incorrect. The author does make it clear that the pharmaceutical industry is not innocent in this situation. However, this isn't an underlying principle; it's more of an expansion on the argument.

Choice *B* is incorrect; the argument does not rely on the principle of harsher punishment for substance abusers; the argument does not even call into question the punishment of these offenders; therefore, Choice *B* is not the best answer.

Choice *D* is incorrect; the argument doesn't claim that the United States is *leading* in terms of drug addiction, only that it is "running rampant throughout the nation." This question is incorrect.

Choice *E* is incorrect. This choice is tempting; however, it is not the *best* answer. The argument does assume that lawmakers can turn the epidemic around based on a certain principle, but it is not the principle of imposing stricter laws on *everyone* involved. Mark this answer as incorrect.

3. A: Choice *A* is the best answer choice here. The original talks about having a skill and working at that skill rather than relying on natural talent to carry through on the success of that skill. Choice *A* also talks about having a skill (athleticism) and working at that skill (practice) in order to have success, rather than relying simply on natural ability to carry through. This is the best answer choice because it is most similar in reasoning to the original passage.

Choice *B* is incorrect; we have something similar to a widespread belief of people about painting just like we had about writing. However, that widespread belief is not eschewed in any way like in the original passage. There is no conflicting belief to the original belief, so this answer choice is incorrect.

Choice *C* is incorrect; although the subject is about writers and writing, the actual *structure* of the passage is different, and thus is incorrect. We don't have a conflicting source of talent like we do in Choice *A* and in the original passage.

Choice *D* is incorrect because it acts more like an informative passage rather than one with a counterargument. We simply are told about the process of becoming a photographer.

Choice *E* is similar to Choice *D* in that it acts more like an informative passage, describing the dangers of bull riding rather than providing a counterargument for a widespread belief.

4. B: Choice *B* is the best answer here; we see the argument mistaking correlation for causation. The arguer knows that the drug PMR had what "would be" negative effects that included complications in childbirth. Then, the arguer ran across an article that showed a rise in complications in childbirth in the same year the drug was being used by the population. The arguer then assumes that the two *must* be related; that the drug PMR was *the cause* of complications during childbirth. However, there is a possibility that this is just an incidence of correlation that the argument failed to account for. We have no way of knowing whether complications during childbirth were a direct effect of the drug or an effect of something else going on in that same year.

5. B: The best answer choice is *B*. Let's look at it in simpler terms: Brown rice contains arsenic. Arsenic can harm the human body by causing cancer and diabetes. Therefore, everyone who eats brown rice will become sick. Or, B contains A. A causes C. Therefore, everyone who eats B will get C. Let's look at the original argument in simpler terms: BN contain S. S causes AI. Therefore, everyone who eats BN will get AI (anti-inflammatory effects). These two arguments are the closest in reasoning as any of the others. Let's look at the rest:

Choice *A* is incorrect because there is no viable argument here. This passage merely explains the nutrients found in cashews and what they do.

Choice *C* is not the correct answer choice because it does not parallel the reasoning in the original passage. Choice *C* says: O does not contain D. Those looking to have D should eat T, M, and S. D is important for C and BG. Not enough D could cause C and WG. This reasoning is much different than what we have in the original paragraph. This is more of an informative passage on Vitamin D rather than a persuasive argument.

Choice *D* also does not parallel the reasoning found in the original passage. Choice *D* says that Whales have lungs instead of gills. Therefore, they use lungs to breathe when they come up from the water. Already our argument looks different than the original "BN contains S. S Causes AI. Therefore, everyone who eats BN will get AI." The passage ends with what everyone should do, mirroring the absolute language, but on the whole the arguments are structured differently.

Choice *E* is close to the correct answer. However, we have a lack of absolutes at the conclusion of the argument: Microwaves contain R. Exposure can cause V, H, and F. Therefore, some who own M may experience V, H, and F. The wording of "some" and "may" provides a different argument structure than Choice *B* and the original passage.

6. D: The correct answer choice is *D*—whether or not modern translation adheres to the beauty of the original text by avoiding a literal rendering of that text. We can see that Jackson believes that modern translation *can* adhere to the beauty of the original text by providing a loose translation, and we see that Hardy disagrees with Jackson and believes that the text must be a literal translation in order to retain the beauty of the text, which lies in the text's meaning.

Choice *A* is incorrect; the passage does not delve into pedagogy or compare modern translation to traditional translation.

Choice *B* is incorrect; Spanish translation is only mentioned to introduce Merwin, and not to act as a point of contention between the two speakers.

Choice *C* is not the best answer here either, as the two do not discuss the future of English translation specifically.

Finally, Choice *E* is incorrect; this would be a good point to bring up if there were a third party listening to Jackson and Hardy arguing; however, this isn't exactly what the two are arguing over in the passage, so we can mark this as incorrect.

7. A: The correct answer is *A*—the examination of popular culture related to theory and its treatment of technology as a replacement for reality is lighthearted enough to focus on in the critical theory teacher's class. The arguer states that Heidegger is far too "serious" to focus on, and in order to study something more playful, they will focus on Baudrillard. This argument, therefore, relies on the assumption that Baudrillard's treatment of technology and pop culture is lighthearted or playful.

Choice *B* is incorrect; this might be an assumption we, as readers, make about the teacher's line of thought, but the teacher's argument does not necessarily require this line of thought.

Choice *C* is incorrect; the teacher's argument is jumbled by the assumption that Heidegger's treatment of language is as important as Baudrillard's treatment of pop culture. The question of importance does not come up in this argument, but rather which topic would be less serious and more fun to work with.

Choice *D* is incorrect; the argument does not rely on the assumption that there are not enough university classes that offer a lighthearted perspective of critical theory. Perhaps a majority of courses focus more on the lighthearted side of theory like this class intends to—whether they do or do not, there is no conclusion leaning either way.

Choice *E* is incorrect; again, there is no assumption underlying the argument on which student is "better" or "worse" off for the study of either philosopher. The assumption has to do with Baudrillard's philosophy of thought being playful and lighthearted.

8. E: The correct answer is Choice *E*. Choice *E* provides a general rule that the original argument abides by (which student to choose for the award). Additionally, it gives us all of the conditions on which the argument relies (talent, effort, and exposure).

Choice *A*: This is incorrect because it leaves out the condition of exposure that the professor takes into consideration.

Choice *B*: This answer choice is incorrect because it leaves the act of gifting an award and replaces the sentiment with who the "better" person is. Whether or not one person is "better" than the other has nothing to do with a talent award to indicate a skill level.

Choice *C*: Choice *C* is incorrect; we have a conditional statement that has to do with measuring skill level in a given position, but this choice leaves out giving an award completely.

Choice *D*: This answer choice is incorrect; notice how the subjects in this choice are plural rather than singular. It mentions "giving awards" in general. An important detail in Choice *E* is that the argument focuses on giving a "single award" to only one person, which drives the difficulty in choosing and brings in the measurement of exposure, skill, and effort. Choice *D* is incorrect because it takes away the condition of having to choose between two people in the action of giving out a single award for talent.

9. C: Choice *C* is the best answer here. Regardless of the new parking lot, if the construction is deterring customers from going into Green Eats Café, then the sales will decrease as a result of this information.

Choice *A* is incorrect; this information would more likely cause the sales to remain the same. It doesn't account for the decrease in sales in the original stem.

Choice *B* is incorrect, though this is a tempting one. Adding parking meters to the lot may deter people from parking there, but we don't know that for sure. Additionally, again, the sales wouldn't decrease as a result of this, because the café didn't have a parking lot to begin with. The sales would more likely stay the same as before the parking lot was added.

Choice *D* is incorrect. Adding stoplights wouldn't deter customers from going into or buying anything at Green Eats Café. If we had more information on this, like, "there was construction from adding the new stoplights," or that people hated the stoplights, we would have more reason to choose this, but otherwise there is not enough information here to justify this choice.

Choice *E* is incorrect because we just don't have enough information here, and the timing is off. The original stem says that the sales decreased *after* the parking lot was built, and here, the flood happened "weeks before" the parking lot was built. Even if the flood did cause extensive damage, we don't have enough information to tell us if that's the case or not.

10. A: Choice *A* is correct; it's the option that best supports the conclusion. The conclusion is that "most of the town's stray cat problem has been solved." Choice *A* provides a solution for the city's cat problem, which is to provide a safe space, food, and vaccinations for stray cats all while allowing them to roam around customers who might adopt them. We also see the percentage of cats that benefit from the café. This statement gets stray cats off the streets, cares for them, and puts them into homes.

Choice *B* is close to the correct answer, but it is missing some important details. The main one is that this choice doesn't have the word "stray" anywhere. Thus, we are not told if the cats are domesticated, specialty cats, or stray cats. The conclusion requires the cats be stray.

Choice *C* is incorrect; we are not told enough information about how this statement has "solved the stray cat problem." The donation jar probably does help stray cats, but we are not told if it has solved the stray cat problem.

Choice *D* is incorrect because it uses the logical fallacy of circular reasoning. The conclusion (the stray cat problem has been solved) is being based on the premise that the stray cat problem has been solved. This still doesn't tell us how the stray cat problem has been solved.

Choice *E* is incorrect. Again, the conclusion is that "the town's stray cat problem has been solved," so we are looking for statements that prove this conclusion is true. The fact that the stray cat problem will continue if Chaucer Café for Cats doesn't keep doing what it's doing might be true, but it doesn't effectively prove the conclusion that "the town's cat problem has been solved."

11. D: Choice *D* correctly identifies the statement that most accurately expresses the publisher's main conclusion. The argument's conclusion is that "publishers need to focus more on the design and interface of digital editions to remain commercially viable." The focus on design and interface are examples of how publishers must adapt to increased demand for digital editions.

Choice *A* is incorrect. The argument characterizes the decline of brick-and-mortar stores as a threat to the publishing industry, but the publisher concludes that the industry can survive by selling more digital editions.

Choice *B* is incorrect. The publisher would definitely agree with this statement, but the conclusion is about how publishers can adapt and capitalize on this room for improvement.

Choice *C* is incorrect. The publisher would agree with this statement, but it's a supporting premise, not the conclusion.

Choice *E* is incorrect. The publisher never mentions whether digital or paper editions are more profitable. Demand for digital books is why publishers need to adapt, not relative profitability.

12. C: Choice *C* correctly identifies an assumption required by the argument. The question is asking for a necessary assumption, meaning that if it weren't true, the argument would fall apart. If there's another type of state exam, then we wouldn't know if all the seniors passed it; thus, we wouldn't know if all the seniors met their graduation requirement to pass all of the state exams.

Choice *A* is incorrect. The passing score is definitely at least 70% since the argument says all of the students passed the exams, but it could be anything lower than 70% without impacting the argument.

Choice *B* is incorrect. The importance of the science exam is irrelevant. The math or literature exam could be the most important, or all three exams could be equally important, and the argument would survive intact.

Choice *D* is incorrect. However, it's very close to being correct. A necessary assumption is that there are *no* other graduation requirements, like the possibility of another state exam. If that were the case, then the argument couldn't conclude that all of the seniors are graduating based solely on the state exam results. But Choice *D* says the argument relies on there being *additional* graduation requirements, which it doesn't.

Choice *E* is incorrect. The conclusion clearly references high school seniors, so the possibility of juniors graduating a year early is irrelevant to the argument.

13. B: Choice *B* correctly identifies the statement most strongly supported by the argument. According to the economist, the country was in a prolonged recession after the job market declined, illustrating how high unemployment can threaten economic health.

Choice *A* is incorrect. The economist mentions numerous obstacles with outsourcing being one of the two examples provided. There's nothing to infer that outsourcing was the *primary* cause.

Choice *C* is incorrect. Although the successful economic reform was bipartisan, there's not enough evidence to infer that bipartisan reform is always the most effective. "Always" goes too far.

Choice *D* is incorrect. The argument doesn't indicate whether automation and outsourcing continue to challenge the economy. If anything, the argument implies they don't, since the economy fully recovered after the bipartisan reform.

Choice *E* is incorrect. The argument says that the economy fully recovered after unemployment dropped to an all-time low, but that's not the same thing as saying it "needed to reach an all-time low." For example, a significant drop in unemployment could have led to an economic recovery.

14. C: Choice *C* correctly identifies the issue in dispute. The salesman is claiming that the commission cap undermines his incentive to work. In contrast, the manager argues that the salesman is incentivized by his base salary and continued employment at the company.

Choice *A* is incorrect. The salesman explicitly says watching videos is a detriment, and the manager threatens to fire the salesman if he watches videos, presumably because it's a detriment.

Choice *B* is incorrect. The salesman is implying his position deserves a special status (uncapped commissions), but the manager compares the salesman's present situation to noncommissioned employees.

Choice *D* is incorrect for the same reason as Choice *A*. Both the salesman and manager would agree that the company would suffer if employees didn't work hard. They disagree over how the employees should be incentivized to work hard.

Choice *E* is incorrect. The salesman believes that a commission cap means he is essentially working for free, but the manager doesn't argue that employees should have to work for free. The manager even mentions the salesman's base salary in his rebuttal.

15. A: Choice *A* correctly identifies the reasoning error that most weakens the argument. The argument is relying on a hasty generalization based on the experiences of a "dozen people." This is the type of insufficient data, typically in the form of anecdotes, that indicates a hasty generalization.

Choice *B* is incorrect. The Drug Enforcement Agency is an appropriate authority to cite when deciding on drug enforcement policy. An inappropriate authority would be irrelevant to the subject matter, like citing the Environmental Protection Agency to defend drug policy.

Choice *C* is incorrect. The Drug Enforcement Agency might have a conflict of interest since criminalizing all drugs would expand the agency's power, but they only called for aggressive action, not universal criminalization like the policymaker. In any event, Choice *A* is more damaging to the policymaker's argument.

Choice *D* is incorrect. The argument mentions neither a probability nor a certainty, let alone confuses the two.

Choice *E* is incorrect. It's true that the policymaker doesn't define "drugs," but it doesn't cause any confusion. In comparison, Choice *A* is a bigger issue for the policymaker.

16. D: Choice *D* correctly identifies the statement that would most strengthen the argument. The argument is that humans should reduce the suffering of conscious beings to zero by universally adopting vegetarianism, and lab-grown meat will encourage more people to change their diet. The ethicist lists the prohibitive cost of a vegetarian diet as an obstacle, and if lab-grown meat were half the cost of animal flesh, then more people would become vegetarianism.

Choice *A* is incorrect. The ethicist isn't concerned with environmental sustainability, only the suffering of conscious beings. As such, it's irrelevant to this argument.

Choice *B* is incorrect. As such, lab-grown meat wouldn't be serving its purpose in the argument if animals suffered in its creation. However, this is a necessary assumption in the ethicist's argument. His entire argument would unravel if lab-grown meat involved the suffering of conscious beings. Although it might strengthen his argument to state this explicitly, it's already part of the argument, so Choice *D* is the stronger answer choice.

Choice *C* is incorrect. This answer choice weakens the argument. If some people eat animal flesh strictly due to its taste, then they might be less likely to adopt vegetarianism by eating only lab-grown meat, even if it were cheaper and provided the same dietary nutrients.

Choice *E* is incorrect. Like Choice *A*, this describes a potential benefit of lab-grown meat that's not related to the ethicist's argument. Ease of regulation might help the lab-grown meat industry in general, but it won't directly encourage people to eat the product and adopt vegetarianism.

17. A: Choice *A* correctly identifies the best resolution to the apparent paradox. The paradox is the company achieving record profits despite declining sales. So, the correct answer will identify a new alternative source of revenue. Licensing designs would be such an alternative, and Choice *A* indicates the company started licensing for the first time last year, effectively resolving the paradox.

Choice *B* is incorrect. Cheaper material might have increased profits by creating a more favorable margin; however, the company also reduced the coats' retail price, presumably for the purpose of increasing sales, which didn't happen.

Choice *C* is incorrect. The company hired marketing and sales consultants last year to help their sales, but the sales still remained at a record low, so this can't explain the paradox.

Choice *D* is incorrect. Although the other manufacturers' struggles might indicate an industry-wide trend, it doesn't explain how the company achieved record profits last year.

Choice *E* is incorrect. This answer would refute what industry insiders think is the reason for low sales, but it doesn't change the fact that sales were at a record low while profits hit a record high.

18. B: Choice *B* correctly identifies a flaw in the argument's reasoning. Circular reasoning is a logical fallacy where a premise and conclusion are indistinguishable. The argument's first sentence illustrates circular reasoning. It's essentially arguing that the Knights are the best, because they're the best.

Choice *A* is incorrect. The only authority the argument cites is Barry Jones who is a professional baseball talent scout. Jones would be an appropriate authority for evaluating a baseball team.

Choice *C* is incorrect. An ad hominem attack is an argument against a person, typically attacking his or her character, rather than against the person's argument. There's no ad hominem argument here.

Choice *D* is incorrect. The argument is that the Knights have a high-powered offense that's outperformed its competition, so they're a contender to win the championship. This isn't self-contradictory.

Choice *E* is incorrect. The argument doesn't make an emotional appeal either in favor of the Knights or against their competition.

19. E: Choice *E* correctly identifies how Willie responds to Xavier's argument. Willie admits the workers' compensation might seem unfair, he adds two pieces of context. First, the dollar's buying power is greater in those countries, so the wages are higher than they appear on paper. Second, these low-paying manufacturing jobs are part of the industrialization process, which helps these countries increase their standard of living in the long-term.

Choice *A* is incorrect. Willie doesn't reject the place of morality. He even argues that overseas manufacturing is moral since it helps those countries industrialize and raise their standard of living.

Choice *B* is incorrect. Willie never addresses Xavier's last point that overseas manufacturing increases demand for temporary products, and therefore, harms the environment.

Choice *C* is incorrect. Willie doesn't claim that industrialization is different in every country. Instead, he argues they're in a different stage of the same industrialization process.

Choice *D* is incorrect. It goes too far by including "solely." Willie has an alternative argument that cheap manufacturing is a necessary stage in the industrialization process.

20. B: Choice *B* correctly identifies the argument that conforms to the principle. The principle is that moral people give without an expectation of receiving something in return. Abraham paid for a random stranger's dinner while traveling in a foreign country, so he gave without expecting anything in return.

Choice *A* is incorrect. Although Christina gave Chelsea something and didn't receive anything in return, the argument doesn't mention her expectations.

Choice *C* is incorrect. A "loan" implies an expectation of repayment, violating the principle from the prompt.

Choice *D* is incorrect. Like Choice *A*, the argument doesn't describe whether Tanya expected anything in return for her generosity.

Choice *E* is incorrect. Although the argument appears to closely mirror the prompt argument, it doesn't mention Holden's state of mind.

21. D: Choice *D* correctly identifies the parallel argument. The prompt argument is that two groups of things are similar when all members of both groups share a single characteristic. Although Choice *D* switches the order of the conclusion and premises, it follows the same logic.

Choice *A* is incorrect. The argument's conclusion differs from the prompt. While there are two different groups that all share one characteristic, the argument concludes that this means that the two groups are the same, rather than merely similar.

Choice *B* is incorrect. The argument doesn't include a conclusion, unlike the prompt argument.

Choice *C* is incorrect. The first clause specifies that only *some* dogs are black. This could mean that only one dog is black, and therefore, the conclusion is much weaker than the prompt argument.

Choice *E* is incorrect. This argument has a different structure than the prompt argument. Instead of making an argument about why two groups of things are similar, Choice *E* argues that since one person shares a characteristic of a group, then he is a member of that group.

22. E: Choice *E* correctly identifies the statement that must be true. Jim opposes a large government, and according to the argument's second sentence, that means he must necessarily favor tax cuts and be moral.

Choice *A* is incorrect. Although most conservatives oppose a large government, Jim could belong to some other political group that holds the same position.

Choice *B* is incorrect. This is necessarily false. Jim opposes large government, and according to the argument, everyone who opposes a large government favors tax cuts.

Choice *C* is incorrect. Jim doesn't necessarily need to be over the age of sixty for two reasons. First, Jim might not be a conservative as described in the explanation for Choice *A*. Second, even if he were a conservative, he might hold a college degree, so he still wouldn't be over the age of sixty.

Choice *D* is incorrect. There's no way to determine Jim's age.

23. D: Choice *D* correctly identifies how the argument proceeds. The scientist is debunking the anti-vaccination movement's argument that vaccines cause illness by providing examples of their effectiveness, identifying precautionary safeguards, and pointing to a lack of evidence. The argument also concludes with a policy proposal—politicians should invest in a public education campaign.

Choice *A* is incorrect. The argument's conclusion is the policy proposal. It doesn't begin with a conclusion that's followed by support.

Choice *B* is incorrect. The argument does list illustrative examples of illness that vaccines have succeeded in fighting, but Choice *B* doesn't fully express how the argument proceeds.

Choice *C* is incorrect. The argument does identify an issue—the anti-vaccination movement—but the scientist argues that if left unchecked, the issue could cause a public health crisis. As such, the scientist doesn't believe the anti-vaccination movement poses a limited risk.

Choice *E* is incorrect. The argument does describe a new phenomenon—the growing anti-vaccination movement—but the scientist doesn't speculate or hypothesize about its cause.

24. B: Choice *B* correctly identifies the most logical conclusion. The line of golf clubs is a new product line. According to the argument, advertisements are most effective with new products; therefore, the golf company should invest in advertisements.

Chapter *A* is incorrect. The company should definitely gain exposure, but the argument is about different ways to generate exposure. Thus, Choice *A* lacks the specificity to most logically complete the argument.

Choice *C* is incorrect. The Internet-based golf supply is new, so it likely doesn't have a lot of preexisting content. As such, search engine optimization wouldn't be the most effective way to gain exposure, especially for a product that's also new.

Choice *D* is incorrect. The argument doesn't describe what situations would be the most optimal to combine advertisements and search engine optimization. In addition, new companies lack the content required to benefit from search engine optimization.

Choice *E* is incorrect. The argument doesn't mention viral marketing strategies at all, and Choice *E* doesn't provide any reason as to why this method would be included for the first time in the conclusion.

25. A: Choice *A* correctly identifies the necessary assumption. The argument is that cell phone companies need to create better batteries, because increased computing power is causing the batteries to die. If the increased computing power didn't strain the battery, there would be no reason for cell phone companies to create them. Thus, Choice *A* is a necessary assumption.

Choice *B* is incorrect. The technician doesn't assume that his current cell phone is defective. If anything, the technician is assuming the opposite—that his current cell phone is representative of other new models.

Choice *C* is incorrect. Like Choice *B*, the technician isn't assuming that his first cell phone was outdated, because he's using it as representative of that generation of cell phone.

Choice *D* is incorrect. The technician seems to believe that computing power will continue to increase. If that happens, then the battery will be even more strained. However, even if computing power stopped growing, cell phone companies would still need to create better batteries to accommodate the existing increase to computing power.

Choice *E* is incorrect. The technician doesn't make a qualitative claim about cell phones, though he would probably agree that increased computing power has improved them. But even if that's the case, his argument doesn't depend on it being true.

26. E: Choice *E* correctly identifies the point of disagreement. Jalen argues that football will never be safe enough to play due to the threat posed by even minor collisions. Liz doesn't dispute that danger, but she argues that players can assume some risk, assuming some precautions are taken.

Choice *A* is incorrect. Jalen explicitly makes this point, and Liz implicitly agrees to it, as evidenced by her proposals for reform, particularly the weight limit and more rigorous drug testing.

Choice *B* is incorrect. Both Jalen and Liz explicitly agree that current football players are risking incurring traumatic brain injuries.

Choice *C* is incorrect. Both Jalen and Liz state that minor collisions can cause brain injury. The difference is that Liz thinks this is an acceptable risk for football players to assume.

Choice *D* is incorrect. Both Jalen and Liz agree that football is inherently dangerous. The difference is that Jalen believes football is too dangerous to play as long as collisions remain part of the game.

27. A: Choice *A* correctly identifies why the argument is vulnerable to criticism. The student is drawing a faulty analogy between law school students and lawyers. Even though the two groups share a similarity— law school students are trying to become lawyers—that doesn't necessarily mean they're similar in other aspects. Lawyers might never need to memorize anything, but law school students could still benefit from developing that skill. The memorization could be intended to help students build a foundation of legal knowledge that all lawyers need.

Choice *B* is incorrect. Begging the question is a type of circular reasoning where the truth of the conclusion is assumed in the premises. The law school student doesn't beg the question.

Choice *C* is incorrect. A red herring distracts from the central issue by raising some irrelevant point. The law school student doesn't introduce a red herring.

Choice *D* is incorrect. The law school student doesn't introduce a cause and effect, so the two aren't confused in the argument.

Choice *E* is incorrect. The law school student says that Professor Lockhart is a demanding teacher, but that's relevant to the argument and not a personal attack. No other person is mentioned in the argument.

28. E: Choice *E* correctly identifies the statement that most logically completes the argument. The argument is that Janet has the strongest possible college application based on merit— valedictorian of the country's top academic high school and a perfect score on the entrance exam—and college admission is exclusively merit-based. The conclusion needs to reflect her impressive accomplishments, and Choice *E* does so.

Choice *A* is incorrect for two reasons. First, the argument never mentions intelligence. Janet could be a mildly intelligent student who worked extremely hard. Second, the argument is clearly steering toward Janet's application and admission to college.

Choice *B* is incorrect. According to the argument, college admission is exclusively merit-based, and volunteer work isn't a merit-based criterion.

Choice *C* is incorrect. Janet will likely be accepted into all of the country's best academic colleges, but she could have reasons to apply elsewhere, like geographic location or cost of tuition. The argument is also focused on Janet's qualifications, not where she's applying.

Choice *D* is incorrect. Janet will likely a strong writer since she earned top grades, but we don't have enough information to conclude her essay will be the *best*. Choice *E* is the most logical conclusion for the argument.

29. C: Choice *C* correctly identifies the most likely point of agreement. Both Alexandra and Zachary believe encouraging children to work hard is important. Alexandra wants to ban participation trophies for this express purpose. Zachary doesn't want to ban participation trophies, but he argues that children will still be encouraged to work hard to win the superior trophy.

Choice *A* is incorrect. Zachary defends participation trophies since they incentivize future participation. In contrast, Alexandra doesn't comment on how participation should be incentivized, if at all.

Choice *B* is incorrect. Zachary argues that participation trophies incentivize future participation, so they presumably don't disappoint children in his view. Alexandra doesn't discuss how children feel about receiving a participation trophy.

Choice *D* is incorrect. Alexandra explicitly agrees that competition should reflect life, but Zachary doesn't connect competition to life lessons in the same way.

Choice *E* is incorrect. Like Choice *D*, Alexandra would agree with this answer, but Zachary doesn't provide his worldview.

30. C: Choice *C* correctly identifies the statement that would most weaken the argument. If most criminals aren't rational actors, then the type of punishment won't be a deterrent. Irrational people don't evaluate the pros and cons, like whether their action could result in a death sentence, before taking some action. Thus, Choice *C* is extremely damaging to the criminologist's argument.

Choice *A* is incorrect. The criminologist's biggest priority is reducing crime, arguing that this would "outweigh all of the death penalty's costs," like executing some innocent people.

Choice *B* is incorrect. Rehabilitation is irrelevant to the criminologist's argument. Even if every criminal could be rehabilitated, the criminologist is arguing that some should still be executed to reduce crime through deterrence.

Choice *D* is incorrect. This doesn't necessarily weaken the criminologist's argument. Even if executions cost more money upfront, the criminologist is arguing that the death penalty would reduce crime overall, and thereby, save the state money in the long run.

Choice *E* is incorrect. The death penalty's unpopularity might make it difficult to pass the criminologist's plan, but it doesn't undermine his substantive argument that the death penalty would be an effective deterrent.

31. C: Choice *C* correctly identifies the statement that would weaken the argument. The argument is that the best breakfast beverage is the one in which the amount of caffeine can be customized in every cup, so instant coffee is the best breakfast beverage, since it is the most customizable. So, the correct answer will explain why some other beverage is similarly customizable. Choice *C* is correct, because it says that tea bags can be combined, allowing for the amount of caffeine to be customized per cup.

Choice *A* is incorrect. Taste is irrelevant. The argument defines the best breakfast beverage solely based on its ability to customize the amount of caffeine per cup.

Choice *B* is incorrect. Although Choice *B* appears to weaken the argument for instant coffee, it's irrelevant for the same reason that Choice *A* is. Instant coffee's taste doesn't impact the argument.

Choice *D* is incorrect. Espresso might have more caffeine than coffee, but Choice *D* doesn't state that espresso's caffeine content is customizable, which is what matters in this argument.

Choice *E* is incorrect. Like taste, health is irrelevant to the argument. The argument is only concerned with customizable caffeine content.

32. A: Choice *A* correctly identifies the argument that parallels the reasoning in the prompt argument. The prompt argument sets up two possibilities and eliminates one possibility, leaving what remains as the conclusion. Choice *A* does the same thing. Cats are either black or white, and since the cat isn't white, it must be black.

Choice *B* is incorrect. It's a statement about what will happen in the future, not an argument. Choice *B* doesn't argue that Lisa will be CEO or CFO by ruling out one of those two possibilities.

Choice *C* is incorrect. Rather than setting up two possibilities, Choice *C* only expresses what Tate would *want* to do if he wasn't already employed as a mailman.

Choice *D* is incorrect. It doesn't rule out one of two possibilities. Instead, Choice *D* ties a characteristic (having a lair) to a position (super villain), states that Chris holds that position, and concludes he must have that characteristic.

Choice *E* is incorrect. Although Choice *E* appears similar to the prompt argument, it includes three possibilities (HR, sales, and accounting) and only rules out one possibility (HR), leaving the other two as potentially true. Nothing can be concluded as a certainty, like the prompt argument and Choice *A*.

33. C: Choice *C* correctly identifies the main point in dispute. The director and critic are arguing about the director's role. The director argues that directors should be allowed to offend people, if that would accurately reflect reality, so the audience can maintain its suspension of disbelief. The critic would argue that this violates the director's social responsibility to avoid offending people.

Choice *A* is incorrect. Both the director and critic would agree that movie audiences suspend their disbelief. This is the director's main point, and the critic acknowledges its existence by claiming that censoring hate speech and racial slurs won't break the audience's disbelief.

Choice *B* is incorrect. This is the critic's main point, and the director would likely also agree. The director isn't claiming that movies aren't offensive, but that offending people is justified to protect the suspension of disbelief.

Choice *D* is incorrect. This isn't the main point in dispute. In addition, both the director and critic imply that they believe this to be true. For the director, creative control is required to structure a universe where an audience can suspend its disbelief. For the critic, the director would need creative control to censor what the critic deems inappropriate.

Choice *E* is incorrect. The critic would agree that movies have enormous cultural relevancy—that's why the critic is calling for self-censorship—but it's unclear whether the director would agree or disagree.

34. D: Choice *D* correctly identifies an argument that conforms to the principle in the prompt. The principle is that a bad action (switching chairs) is justified when the object was obtained under the same nefarious circumstances (switching chairs without asking). In Choice *D*, Phillip steals a book from someone who obtained that same book through theft.

Choice *A* is incorrect. Tyler commits a bad act (cheating on his taxes), but the government hasn't committed that same bad act.

Choice *B* is incorrect. Diana is committing a bad act (theft) in retribution for some alleged wrong (overcharging). For Choice *B* to be correct, the store would've needed to steal the loaf of bread from a baker or some other party.

Choice *C* is incorrect. Although Choice *C* appears to be similar, it doesn't say whether Abe obtained his seat under similarly nefarious circumstances, like if Abe had originally switched his seat before Mary took it.

Choice *E* is incorrect. Tanya committed a bad act (eating Samantha's sandwich), but the sandwich wasn't obtained under nefarious circumstances.

35. B: Choice *B* correctly identifies the statement that best completes the argument. The argument is that the economy is increasingly dependent on the Internet, so if regulations harm the Internet, then the economy will suffer. Choice *B* accurately expresses where the argument is headed.

Choice *A* is incorrect. The economist is clearly heading toward a conclusion where the regulations harm the economy, but Choice *A* goes too far. It's not clear whether the harm will be so severe that it causes a depression. Choice *B* is more logical.

Choice *C* is incorrect. The economist would probably agree that if the regulation harms the Internet, then physical stores would benefit. However, *dominates* goes too far, and the conclusion would likely address the overall threat to the economy.

Choice *D* is incorrect. Like Choice *C*, the economist would likely agree with Choice *D*, but it doesn't address the overall threat to the economy.

Choice *E* is incorrect. Choice *B* better completes the argument since it addresses the regulation's overall impact, while Choice *E* is limited to one aspect. In addition, *collapse* goes too far, like *dominates* in Choice *C*.

36. A: Choice *A* correctly identifies the flaw in the argument's reasoning. The argument confuses a necessary and sufficient condition. A necessary condition is something that needs to happen to achieve something. It doesn't mean that something will be achieved or obtained; rather, the necessary condition needs to be fulfilled for the result to be possible. A student taking the entrance exam is a necessary condition. Otherwise, the student couldn't ever be accepted into college. A sufficient condition is something that guarantees a result. In this scenario, earning a high score would be a sufficient condition for college admission. Molly satisfied the necessary condition (sitting for the exam), but it's presented as a sufficient condition (scoring high enough to be admitted). Ms. Wilson's speculation isn't enough to turn the necessary condition into a sufficient condition.

Choice *B* is incorrect. The argument doesn't use one term in two different ways.

Choice *C* is incorrect. The argument doesn't fail to define an important term. The most important term is the exam, and it's defined in the argument.

Choice *D* is incorrect. The only authority cited is Ms. Wilson, and she teaches an exam preparation class, so she's in an appropriate position to comment on her students' potential for success.

Choice *E* is incorrect. The argument doesn't make a hasty generalization, which is drawing a conclusion off limited evidence, typically presented as an anecdote.

37. D: Choice *D* correctly identifies the argument's conclusion. The argument concedes that the atomic bombs had a tragic consequence (civilian deaths) but justifies their use due to the estimated cost of the alternative (invasion). Choice *D* correctly expresses the historian's conclusion that the atomic bombs were the least bad option available.

Choice *A* is incorrect. The last sentence is a red herring. Although the Japanese committed war crimes, the main conclusion isn't that those war crimes meant they deserved to be bombed with nuclear weapons. Instead, those war crimes function as an additional premise.

Choice *B* is incorrect. Although Japan's refusal to surrender factored into America's strategic calculations, *forced* goes too far. Choice *D* is a more accurate expression of the historian's conclusion.

Choice *C* is incorrect. The historian doesn't argue that the decision was easy, as evidenced by the inclusion of the atomic weapon's civilian death toll.

Choice *E* is incorrect. Like Choice *B*, Japan's inevitable defeat was a factor in the United States' calculations, not the historian's conclusion.

38. E: Choice *E* correctly identifies a point of agreement between the trainer and nutritionist. The trainer argues that cardio and weight lifting help sustain weight loss to prevent heart disease, the country's leading cause of death. The nutritionist argues that a healthy diet is the foundation for the weight loss necessary to prevent heart disease. Thus, both the trainer and nutritionist would agree that some people would benefit from losing weight.

Choice *A* is incorrect. Neither the trainer nor nutritionist address whether weight loss or building muscle is more important.

Choice *B* is incorrect. The nutritionist contends that exercise must be accompanied by a healthy diet, but the trainer doesn't mention a diet at all. So, it's unclear whether the trainer would agree.

Choice *C* is incorrect. The trainer states that cardio and weightlifting can lower resting heart rate. The caloric deficit isn't directly linked to lowering resting heart rate. In addition, the nutritionist doesn't mention heart rate at all.

Choice *D* is incorrect. Although this seems like a reasonable statement that a hypothetical trainer and nutritionist might agree on, neither the trainer nor the nutritionist in this question address how different people have different needs.

39. E: Choice *E* correctly identifies the statement that best resolves the apparent paradox. The paradox is that food production is at a record high, but an unprecedented number of people died from starvation. Choice *E* explains the paradox by stating that the population is growing even faster than the food production, causing many people to starve.

Choice *A* is incorrect. If the increase in food production was limited to simple carbohydrates, it might not be ideal, perhaps even causing malnutrition, but it wouldn't explain starvation.

Choice *B* is incorrect. Subsistence agriculture doesn't explain why people are starving when food production is so high. An additional fact is needed here, like subsistence agriculture being a group of people's only access to food.

Choice *C* is incorrect. It lacks a connection between family farms and access to food, like subsistence farming's role in Choice *B*.

Choice *D* is incorrect. Income inequality might limit some people's access to food, but it doesn't necessarily mean that more people will starve to death. For example, income inequality might be growing due to the ultra-wealthy accumulating more money while the rest of the population experiences stagnant growth. Choice *E* more directly addresses the paradox.

40. B: Choice *B* correctly identifies a statement that the ethicist would agree with. The ethicist is troubled by the lack of incentives for private companies to regulate artificial intelligence. According to the ethicist's conclusion, artificial intelligence is adopting humanity's worst impulses and violent worldviews, and thereby threatening humanity.

Choice *A* is incorrect. The ethicist might agree that artificial intelligence is negatively impacting society, but the Internet is barely mentioned in this argument. It's unclear whether the ethicist believes that the Internet's influence on artificial intelligence makes the Internet have a negative impact on society.

Choice *C* is incorrect. Although the ethicist would likely agree with this general sentiment, Choice *C* is too broad. The argument is limited to artificial intelligence, not technological advancement generally, and it's unclear whether the ethicist would *always* take this position in those additional scenarios.

Choice *D* is incorrect. The ethicist doesn't argue for limiting artificial intelligence to simple algorithms. The problem isn't the advancement; it's that the artificial intelligence's growth isn't aligned with humanity's interest, according to the ethicist.

Choice *E* is incorrect. The ethicist never mentions civil rights, so there's nothing that implies that the ethicist would apply those rights to artificial intelligence.

41. C: Choice *C* correctly identifies why the argument is most vulnerable to criticism. The argument asserts a conspiracy theory, and when a government spokesman rejects it, the argument attacks the spokesman's character, rather than offering a substantive rebuttal. Thus, it is an ad hominem argument.

Choice *A* is incorrect. The argument is not from authority. An argument from authority claims that something is true based on an authority figure simply declaring it so.

Choice *B* is incorrect. The argument doesn't rely on an emotional appeal.

Choice *D* is incorrect. The argument doesn't introduce a red herring. A red herring is something that is intentionally misleading, serving as a distraction from the argument.

Choice *E* is incorrect. The argument doesn't include a slippery slope. A slippery slope is a claim that some action or event will spiral into a series of even worse actions and/or events.

42. E: Choice *E* correctly identifies a necessary assumption in the argument. If video games cannot be played on cell phones, then the problem wouldn't be getting worse due to children's increased access to violent video games. Without this assumption being true, the psychologist's central premise and conclusion would be undermined.

Choice *A* is incorrect. The argument doesn't depend on violent video games being unpopular ten years ago. It's more focused on the future and never mentions when violent video games first became popular. Violent video games could've become popular the year before, and the psychologist's argument would be the same.

Choice *B* is incorrect. If children didn't naturally play aggressively, the psychologist's argument might be strengthened since violent video games would be the sole cause of any aggression. However, the psychologist's argument is the same even if violent video games are only adding to the existing aggression.

Choice *C* is incorrect. The psychologist doesn't need to assume that the government is legally obligated to prevent crime. Whether legally obligated or not, the psychologist could still argue that the government should prevent violent crimes. The argument doesn't depend on the existence of this being an obligation.

Choice *D* is incorrect. The psychologist mentions graphic depictions of gun violence being especially dangerous, but the argument is concerned with aggressive interactions, not the children actually using guns. Whether the children have access to guns isn't an assumption; in fact, it's irrelevant.

43. B: Choice *B* correctly identifies a statement that must follow from the passage. The government will only invest in alternative energy sources when the Green Party controls 51 seats, and they only control 22 seats. So, in the current legislative session, the country will go bankrupt, and as a result, will not be able to fund its military.

Choice *A* is incorrect. The passage states that extreme weather events will bankrupt the government, but it doesn't claim that the cost *per* extreme weather event will increase. The bankruptcy could be caused by an increased frequency in extreme weather events.

Choice *C* is incorrect. The passage states that 60 Green Party politicians are projected to win seats in the upcoming election, and this would theoretically trigger an investment in alternative energy during the next legislative session. However, 60 Green Party politicians in the legislature is only a projection; it's not necessarily true.

Choice *D* is incorrect. There are only 22 Green Party politicians in the legislature; therefore, the threat of climate change won't be mitigated during this legislative session.

Choice *E* is incorrect. Voters might support making the investment since 60 Green Party politicians are projected to win in the upcoming elections. But we don't know if that's why they support the Green Party. It's possible that some other position or opposition to incumbents is driving the Green Party's increased popularity.

44. D: Choice *D* correctly identifies the only statement that wouldn't weaken the argument. If students pursuing online degrees don't need to commute, they would save money on transportation costs and have more time to study. This would strengthen the argument, not weaken it.

Choice *A* is incorrect. Online students would miss this opportunity to attend networking events on campus, so it weakens the argument that online colleges are superior.

Choice *B* is incorrect. If online colleges have less structural support and resources, then it hurts the argument that online colleges are superior to the in-person experience.

Choice *C* is incorrect. The argument claims that the world's best colleges offer online courses, but if those credits can't be applied toward a degree without attending the physical college in person, then their functional value is diminished, weakening the argument.

Choice *E* is incorrect. If employers don't value online college degrees, then the degree itself loses value, undermining the argument.

45. D: Choice *D* correctly identifies the statement that must be true. Jonathan is a wealthy person, and no wealthy person owns less than two homes. Therefore, Jonathan must own at least two homes.

Choice *A* is incorrect. Although Jonathan is wealthy, some wealthy people haven't worked hard (those born into wealthy families).

Choice *B* is incorrect. It's not necessarily true that Jonathan is from a wealthy family. The argument leaves open the possibility of a poor person becoming wealthy through hard work.

Choice *C* is incorrect. There's no indication that Jonathan grew up in a poor family. As mentioned above, Jonathan could've grown up poor and become wealthy through hard work, but that's not necessarily true.

Choice *E* is incorrect. Jonathan is a wealthy person. According to the argument, only some poor people can't afford to pay rent.

46. B: Choice *B* correctly identifies the best investment opportunity. The cardinal rule has three requirements—privately held small business, sells tangible goods, and no debt. Elizabeth's store is a privately held small business (standalone and owned by her), it sells tangible goods (board games), and it has no debt. The lack of profitability is irrelevant, acting as a red herring. The cardinal rule doesn't mention it, presumably since the businessman thinks he can increase profitability as long as the business meets those three requirements.

Choice *A* is incorrect. Jose's grocery store owes the bank three months' worth of mortgage payments, so it has debt, violating the cardinal rule.

Choice *C* is incorrect. The accounting firm violates the cardinal rule, because it does not sell a tangible good.

Choice *D* is incorrect. A multinational corporation is not a small business, so it violates the cardinal rule.

Choice *E* is incorrect. The regional chain of liquor stores has debt (small business loan), so it's a worse investment than the board game store according to the businessman's cardinal rule.

47. A: Choice *A* correctly identifies the argument's primary purpose. The purpose is clearly persuasive, and the focus is on the newspaper's approach to journalism. According to the conclusion, the newspaper isn't currently meeting basic editorial standards, and the journalist wants the newspaper to adopt the best practices described in the argument.

Choice *B* is incorrect. The journalist mentions that the newspaper is currently exposed to charges of bias from all sides, but the argument isn't defending the newspaper. It's calling for a change in editorial policy.

Choice *C* is incorrect. Although the journalist might agree that the newspaper needs to shake up its staff, the primary focus is on the newspaper's approach to journalism.

Choice *D* is incorrect. The journalist touches on the professional responsibilities of a journalist, but it's in the context of the newspaper's failings, which Choice *D* doesn't reference.

Choice *E* is incorrect. The journalist isn't explaining the newspaper's editorial standards. Instead, the argument is describing the ideal editorial standard and calling for the newspaper to adopt it into practice.

48. C: Choice *C* correctly identifies a necessary assumption in the argument. The argument is that hunting licenses for endangered species should be sold to support conservation efforts. If the revenue from those licenses isn't funding conservation efforts, then the ecologist's entire argument falls apart.

Choice *A* is incorrect. Hunting licenses for non-endangered species could be profitable, and the ecologist's argument wouldn't be impacted one way or another. The ecologist could still argue that hunting licenses should be expanded to further increase funding for species that are still endangered.

Choice *B* is incorrect. The ecologist would definitely agree that all one hundred animal species should be saved, but it isn't a necessary assumption. The argument would function the same if the ultimate goal were to save ten endangered animal species.

Choice *D* is incorrect. Like Choice *B*, the ecologist would agree that conservation efforts should've begun earlier, but it isn't a necessary assumption.

Choice *E* is incorrect. The ecologist likely supports hunting licenses for endangered species due to old and lame animals' diminished capacity to reproduce. But reproduction being physically impossible isn't a necessary assumption. The argument would be the same even if those animals were reproducing on a limited basis.

49. A: Choice *A* correctly identifies the statement that most strengthens the argument. The argument is that the city must ban smoking, because every cigarette that's smoked costs the city $1,000. Choice *A* eliminates a possible counterargument for a less extreme measure—taxing tobacco. Since the tax didn't work, the city would be more likely to pursue a total ban.

Choice *B* is incorrect. If smoking cigarettes was already banned in bars and restaurants, it might strengthen the argument by laying the foundation for a total ban. However, a total ban is much more extreme, and Choice *A* is stronger since it eliminates a primary counterargument against changing the law.

Choice *C* is incorrect. Non-smoking related pollution in the waterways and airways might increase the need to avoid additional pollutants, but it's not as strong as Choice *A*.

Choice *D* is incorrect. The existence of tobacco substitutes doesn't justify banning tobacco. It also doesn't necessarily mean that they'll be better for the healthcare system and environment.

Choice *E* is incorrect. The state government's decision to ban tobacco could encourage the city government to do the same, but Choice *A* has a more direct impact on that debate as it pertains to the city.

50. E: Choice *E* correctly identifies a statement that must be true. The passage says it's Monday, so John isn't visiting his lawyer. The contrapositive of "If John is on the green line, he's visiting his lawyer" is "If John doesn't visit his lawyer, then John won't take the green line." The contrapositive (flipping and negating a conditional statement) is always true. Thus, John won't be taking the green line on Monday.

Choice *A* is incorrect. Other than the reference to the red line, the passage doesn't specify when John goes to the doctor. Since it's unclear whether John is taking the red line, John may or may not go to the doctor on Monday.

Choice *B* is incorrect for the same reason as Choice *A*.

Choice *C* is incorrect. The passage says John treats himself to ice cream after he visits the doctor's office, but as explained above, it's unclear whether John is visiting his doctor. Thus, it's also unclear whether he's treating himself to ice cream on Monday.

Choice *D* is incorrect. The passage doesn't include any information that indicates whether or not John is taking the red line on Monday.

LSAT Analytical Reasoning

The Analytical Reasoning section of the LSAT is intended to assess the deductive capabilities of the test taker by presenting a scenario that must adhere to certain conditions or rules. The test taker must then answer questions to determine if they have appropriately understood and applied those conditions. The prompts are not necessarily based on law topics. However, the skills used to solve these problems are also necessary to work through law issues based on a variety of laws and regulations. Situations like cases involving complicated contract terms or cases with contradicting facts can require similar logic and reasoning to the logic problems presented on this section of the LSAT.

The premise and parameters usually require either grouping, matching, ordering, or a combination of the three. The test taker must analyze the parameters to determine the relationship or possible relationships that exist between the persons, things, or events discussed in the premise. Each premise will have a set of questions that address it. Examples of prompts include the seating arrangements for a dinner party, the order of subjects taught at school, and matching employees to job titles and duties.

The types of problems in the Analytical Reasoning section test for the following skills:

- Understanding structure

- Analyzing if/then statements

- Inferring possibilities

- Comprehending rules of logic

Understanding Structure

Recognizing the different structures of the puzzles used in this section can give additional insight into solving them. All the games involve placing elements in positions or relationships. In grouping type problems, the test taker will be asked to place the variables into two or three categories like putting people on teams or doing chores on certain days of the week. Sometimes the number of variables in each category are fixed, but other times, they are not. When working through a matching type problem, there are two sets of variables, but they will not be put into a particular order. Rather, the two sets of variables will be matched together like people and the types of homes they live in or restaurants and their featured dishes. Ordering, or sequencing, type games involve assigning the elements provided into set spots using a 1:1 ratio. For example, a sequencing problem may require the test taker to find the correct order for seven plays to compete in a competition with seven spots.

Analyzing If/Then Statements

If/then statements are a common type of rule presented in analytical reasoning exercises. These statements consist of two pieces of information that relate or connect to each other. If A, then B, with A and B being conditions. Therefore, if condition A occurs, then condition B must also occur. These types of statements can be further classified as fixed or variable. An example of a fixed if/then statement would be, if John buys the green shoes, then Judy will buy the red shoes. There is only one way to apply these two conditions. The following is an example of a variable statement: If John buys the green shoes, then Judy will buy either the red shoes or the blue shoes. The second condition is not fixed. Another type of condition sometimes found in these puzzles is an either/or statement, which suggests two alternative scenarios. Either the school will get the grant, or the library will get the grant.

Inferring Possibilities

Understanding the rules presented in the logic puzzles and deciphering how they come together will help determine the possible outcomes of the situations given. Inferences are arrived at after examining the evidence (in this case, the information from the prompt and the conditions) and applying reasoning. Generally, inferences are made based on which statements are most supported by the system of information given. Sometimes, rules clearly state parts of the solution, but other times, the test taker must consider the deeper implications of each condition. It is not necessary to ascertain the complete sequence or match up of test items as there are often multiple correct combinations.

Comprehending Rules of Logic

Completing the Analytical Reasoning section of the LSAT requires a solid foundation in logic rules and theories. Test takers must be familiar with different logical indicator words and conditional statements. If/then statements were previously discussed, but test takers should also be able to recognize contrapositives, compound statements, and logically equivalent statements. Contrapositives occur when the conditions in an if/then statement take on the opposite meaning. Contrapositives have the form if not A, then not B. If/then statements can be converted to contrapositives to glean additional information. Compound statements contain two or more logic operations. For example, if Ron is stressed or tired, he will bite his nails. This compound statement provides two truths. One, if Ron is stressed, he will bite his nails. Two, if Ron is tired, he will bite his nails. Other logically equivalent statements can be derived by substituting information with the same meaning into different rules and conditions to arrive at additional solutions.

Reading the Passage Carefully

A careful reading of the prompt and the conditions is the first step to comprehending the necessary information to solve these problems and identifying the type of structure being used. The type of structure will help determine where and how the other information will fit together. Once the type of problem is identified, the conditions and questions can be read. When reading the conditions, it is important to interpret the rules correctly. Test takers must be careful not to read additional information into the conditions that is not warranted. The conditions are not meant to be tricky; they are intended to be taken at face value. Finding additional implications based on logical reasoning is part of the process, but not assuming other truths based on where something is presented in the condition or outside information not specifically mentioned in the text.

Question Independence

The next step is to read the question. The question may give additional rules that apply only to that question. This may require drawing a question-specific diagram or making a notation to reinforce that rule. The answer choices must be examined to see which do not conform to the given rules and regulations. This can often be done by using the original diagram created or by making additional inferences based on that particular question. It is also important to treat and answer each question independently. Only the original rules and prompt should be applied to every question that relates to that prompt. Test takers must be mindful of question wording, as the language is usually very specific and determining what the question is asking for will be key to arriving at the correct answer.

Highlighting Text and Using Diagrams

Highlighting or noting important information can help with synthesizing and remembering crucial details. Many test takers find it helpful to create a diagram that represents the description of the scenario with places for conclusions and assumptions to be entered in. This can give the test taker a clear visual picture of the information presented and where deduction is necessary to fill in the blanks. Effectively visualizing the relationships inherent in the rules of the game will assist in answering questions quickly and clearly.

Sample Questions

The following are some examples of the types of prompts, conditions, and questions that are included on the Analytical Reasoning section of the test.

Passage 1

Six students are practicing a musical solo at today's rehearsal. To accommodate the students' schedule and the instrument availability, the following rules must be followed:

- The drum solo must be rehearsed after the tuba solo.
- The flute and the guitar are practiced one directly after the other.
- The piano cannot be played in the first or second rehearsal spot.
- The violin is practiced second.

1. Which of the following could be the order of the rehearsal?
    a. violin, drum, flute, guitar, tuba, piano
    b. tuba, violin, flute, guitar, drum, piano
    c. piano, violin, tuba, guitar, flute, drum
    d. tuba, flute, violin, guitar, piano, drum
    e. violin, piano, tuba, guitar, flute, drum

1. B: The order of tuba, violin, flute, guitar, drum, and piano could be the order of the rehearsal because it does not break any of the rules provided. Choice A could not be correct because the violin must be practiced in the second spot. Also, the drum solo must be rehearsed after the tuba solo, not before. Choice C is not the correct order because the piano cannot be rehearsed in the first or second rehearsal spot. Choice D is not correct because the flute and the guitar should be practiced directly after one another. Also, this choice does not have the violin listed in the second spot as it needs to be. Choice E is not the correct order because the violin is not practiced second and the piano is played in the second spot. Both of these are violations of the listed conditions.

2. If the flute must be played after the drum, which of the following could be true?
    a. The flute could be played in the fourth spot.
    b. The flute could be played in the third spot.
    c. The flute could be played before the violin.
    d. The flute could be played before the tuba.
    e. The flute could be played between the drum and the piano.

2. A: If the flute must be played after the drum, then the flute could be played in the fourth spot. A possible rehearsal schedule that incorporates this new rule with the original rules is tuba, violin, drum, flute, guitar, and piano. Choice B would be impossible because the tuba comes before the drum, and the violin must be in the second spot. So, the earliest the flute could be played is in the fourth spot. Choice C could not be true because the violin must be played in the second spot, and as stated previously, the

earliest the flute could be played is the fourth spot. Choice D is incorrect because the flute could not be played before the tuba. The flute must be played after the drum, and according to the original rules, the drum must be played after the tuba. Choice E is incorrect because the flute and the guitar must be played directly after one another to follow the original rules.

Passage 2
A group of coworkers—Hal, Seth, Claire, Joan, Ethan, and Zoe—attend a meeting. They all sit at a round table in the conference room. There seating arrangement adheres to the following conditions:

- Joan must sit between Claire and Ethan.
- Seth cannot sit beside Ethan.
- If Zoe sits next to Claire, then she does not sit next to Hal.

1. Which of the following is a possible seating arrangement for the meeting?
    a. Joan, Hal, Ethan, Seth, Zoe, Claire
    b. Claire, Joan, Ethan, Seth, Hal, Zoe
    c. Ethan, Joan, Claire, Hal, Zoe, Seth
    d. Hal, Seth, Zoe, Claire, Joan, Ethan
    e. Ethan, Claire, Seth, Zoe, Hal, Joan

1. D: A possible seating arrangement that meets all the conditions in the passage is Hal, Seth, Zoe, Claire, Joan, Ethan. In this arrangement, Joan is between Claire and Ethan, which adheres to the first rule. Seth is not next to Ethan, which abides by the second rule. Zoe is next to Claire, but not Hal, which means that the third rule is also satisfied. Choice A is not a possible seating arrangement because Joan is not between Claire and Ethan, and Seth is sitting next to Ethan. Choice B is does not meet the conditions because Seth is next to Ethan, and Zoe is seated next to Hal and Claire. Choice C is not correct because Seth and Ethan are next to each other due to the round table configuration. Choice E is not a possible seating arrangement because Joan is not sitting between Claire and Ethan.

2. If Ethan is between Joan and Zoe, which of the following could be true?
    a. Claire is sitting next to Zoe.
    b. Seth cannot sit next to Hal.
    c. Claire is sitting between Joan and Seth.
    d. Claire is sitting between Seth and Hal.
    e. Joan is sitting next to Seth.

2. C: The statement that could be true is that Claire is sitting between Joan and Seth. This does not violate the conditions in the prompt and aligns with the additional information that Ethan is sitting between Joan and Zoe. Choice A is not correct because Claire must be sitting next to Joan who is sitting on one side of Ethan with Zoe on the other. Choice B is not supported by any of the conditions. Choice D is not true because Claire must be next to Joan so she cannot have Hal and Seth on each side of her. Choice E is incorrect because Joan must sit between Claire and Ethan.

Passage 3
Four men visit a local flower shop to buy flowers for Valentine's Day. Sam, Dave, Jeff, and Kyle must choose from roses, lilies, daisies, or tulips. They must then choose a vase for their flowers from a selection of red, pink, clear, and silver vases. Each man picks one type of flower and one vase with no overlapping choices.

Their purchases are consistent with the following:

- Sam does not choose roses or a clear vase.
- Jeff purchases daisies.
- If Dave picks a silver vase, then Kyle must pick the red vase.
- Neither Kyle nor Jeff chooses tulips.
- The man who purchases roses chooses the silver vase.

1. If Dave purchases a silver vase, what color vase and flowers does Sam choose?
   a. Pink, tulips
   b. Red, tulips
   c. Clear, lilies
   d. Pink, roses
   e. Red, daisies

1. A: A table or diagram can be used to determine what vase and flowers Sam chose. The conditions can be used to fill in the information in the table. 1. If Dave purchased the silver vase, he also purchased the roses. 2. If Dave picked the silver vase, then Kyle must have picked the red vase. 3. Sam did not choose the clear vase, so the only other color vase left that he could pick is the pink. 4. Because there is only the clear vase left, that means Jeff chose the clear vase. 5. Jeff purchased the daisies. 6. Kyle did not choose tulips, so the only flower left he could have chosen is the lilies. 7. The only type of flower still remaining is the tulips, so Sam must have purchases the tulips. The table below shows the information recorded for each step in the problem-solving process.

Man	Vase	Flower
Sam	3. Pink	7. Tulips
Dave	1. Silver	1. Roses
Jeff	4. Clear	5. Daisies
Kyle	2. Red	6. Lilies

2. Which of the following could be true?
   a. Jeff purchases the silver vase.
   b. Sam chooses daisies.
   c. Kyle purchases the red vase and the tulips.
   d. Sam picks the silver vase.
   e. Dave chooses the clear vase and the tulips.

2. E: The only choice that can be true is that Dave chooses the clear vase and the tulips. Choice A is incorrect because if Jeff purchased the silver vase, he would have also purchased roses, not daisies. Choice B is not true because Jeff chose the daisies, so Sam cannot. Choice C is incorrect because the conditions state Kyle did not choose tulips. Choice D cannot be true because if Sam purchases the silver vase, he would have to purchase roses, but the conditions state that he did not.

Practice Questions

Use the following problem for questions 1-5:

A company is looking to hire three new employees from a group of six applicants. The applicants are Larry, Vanessa, Clarissa, Dimitri, Mark, and Aaron. They must also use the following conditions when making their decision:

- They must hire at least one male and one female.
- If they hire two females, then they must hire Aaron as the male.
- Aaron cannot work with Mark.
- If Mark is selected, then they must select Vanessa.
- Dimitri, Larry, and Clarissa cannot work together in any combination.

1. Which of the following is an acceptable combination of hires?
   a. Dimitri, Mark, and Aaron
   b. Vanessa, Mark, and Clarissa
   c. Larry, Vanessa, and Mark
   d. Mark, Clarissa, and Larry
   e. Clarissa, Aaron, and Mark

2. How many different combinations of hires can be made if it is known that Dimitri will be hired?
   a. 1
   b. 2
   c. 3
   d. 4
   e. 5

3. If Clarissa is hired, which of the following is a permissible team?
   a. Clarissa, Dimitri, Aaron
   b. Clarissa, Vanessa, Mark
   c. Clarissa, Aaron, Mark
   d. Clarissa, Larry, Aaron
   e. Clarissa, Vanessa, Aaron

4. If the first rule was removed so that instead of needing at least one male and one female per team the team was to include only male applicants, how many possible team combinations would there be?
   a. 0
   b. 1
   c. 2
   d. 3
   e. 4

5. How many total team combinations are possible while still satisfying all of the given conditions?
   a. 1
   b. 2
   c. 3
   d. 4
   e. 5

Use the following problem for questions 6-10:

A middle school is having tryouts for the basketball team. The coach is trying to pick the final two spots for a small forward and point guard. The choices that remain are Derek, Shaun, Clayton, Xavier, Thomas, and Hector. The following conditions also apply:

- Hector can only play small forward.
- Xavier and Derek are the only players that can play both positions.
- Xavier, Thomas, and Hector cannot be cannot be picked together in any combination.
- If Derek is picked, then neither Shaun nor Clayton can be picked.
- If Derek is picked for point guard, then he cannot play with Xavier.

6. If the coach picks Xavier for small forward, which of the following contains all the other players he could pick?
   a. Derek, Hector, or Clayton
   b. Clayton or Shaun
   c. Derek, Thomas, or Hector
   d. Derek or Hector
   e. Clayton, Shaun, or Hector

7. If Derek is picked for point guard, who could possibly be picked for small forward?
   a. Shaun or Clayton
   b. Xavier, Thomas, or Clayton
   c. Thomas or Clayton
   d. Thomas or Hector
   e. Hector or Xavier

8. If Derek is selected for point guard, which of the following choices contains all of the players that can be chosen for small forward?
   a. Hector only
   b. Hector or Thomas only
   c. Hector or Shaun only
   d. Thomas or Shaun only
   e. Hector, Thomas, or Shaun only

9. If Shaun is selected, which of the following players cannot be his teammate?
   a. Thomas
   b. Xavier
   c. Clayton
   d. Derek
   e. Hector

10. If Xavier gets injured during tryouts, how many viable pairs can fill the two slots on the team?
   a. 5
   b. 6
   c. 7
   d. 8
   e. 9

Use the following problem for questions 11-15:

A teacher is having her students bring healthy snacks to share at snack time each day. One student per day will bring the class snack from Monday, May 12 – Friday, May 16. The students that will bring snacks are Jessica, Wade, Victor, Chelsea, and Riley. Wade and Chelsea will be using blenders to prepare their snacks. The following conditions also apply:

- Victor must bring snacks after Jessica.
- Chelsea must bring snacks sometime between Wade and Jessica.
- Blenders cannot be used on Tuesday.
- Riley must bring the class snack on Tuesday or Wednesday.

11. Which of the following is a possible order for the students to provide snacks?
    a. Jessica, Riley, Victor, Wade, Chelsea
    b. Jessica, Victor, Riley, Wade, Chelsea
    c. Wade, Chelsea, Riley, Jessica, Victor
    d. Jessica, Victor, Riley, Chelsea, Wade
    e. Wade, Victor, Riley, Chelsea, Jessica

12. Which of the following lists all of the students that could possibly bring snack for the class on Friday?
    a. Wade, Victor, or Chelsea
    b. Victor or Jessica
    c. Wade or Jessica
    d. Victor, Wade, or Jessica
    e. Victor or Wade

13. If it is determined that Victor provides snacks on Wednesday, then what day must Wade bring snack?
    a. Monday
    b. Tuesday
    c. Wednesday
    d. Thursday
    e. Friday

14. If blenders now must be used on Tuesday, how many possible orders of the students exist?
    a. 0
    b. 1
    c. 2
    d. 3
    e. 4

15. If Wade is going to be out of town on Monday, what days can he possibly bring the class snack?
    a. Tuesday and Thursday only
    b. Thursday and Friday only
    c. Friday only
    d. Tuesday, Thursday, and Friday only
    e. Thursday only

Use the following problem to answer questions 16-20:

A history teacher is scheduling her students' presentation order for a given day. There are seven students who need to present individually—Brenda, Carlos, Duane, Felicity, Greg, Harold, and Jackie—and she is putting them in slots numbered one to seven. The assignment of the order of student presentations is subject to the following restrictions:

- Jackie and Harold cannot be assigned to consecutive slots.
- Brenda must present earlier than Jackie.
- Duane must present later than Greg.
- If Greg does not present fourth, then Felicity must.
- Brenda and Duane's assignments must be in consecutive time slots.

16. Which of the following could be a possible order that the students present?
    a. Brenda, Duane, Felicity, Greg, Harold, Carlos, Jackie
    b. Carlos, Harold, Brenda, Greg, Duane, Jackie, Felicity
    c. Greg, Brenda, Duane, Felicity, Harold, Carlos, Jackie
    d. Greg, Duane, Brenda, Felicity, Jackie, Harold, Carlos
    e. Greg, Harold, Duane, Brenda, Felicity, Jackie, Carlos

17. If Brenda presents third, then which of the following must be true?
    a. Jackie presents seventh.
    b. Duane presents first.
    c. Greg presents fourth.
    d. Harold presents second.
    e. Carlos presents sixth.

18. Which of the following could be true?
    a. Brenda is assigned to the first time slot.
    b. Duane is assigned to the fifth time slot.
    c. Harold is assigned to the sixth time slot.
    d. Greg is assigned to the seventh time slot.
    e. Jackie is assigned to the third time slot.

19. If Carlos presents third, then each of the following could be true EXCEPT:
    a. Brenda presents fifth.
    b. Duane presents sixth.
    c. Felicity presents fourth.
    d. Harold presents first.
    e. Jackie presents second.

20. If Harold presents seventh, then who must present fifth?
    a. Brenda
    b. Carlos
    c. Duane
    d. Jackie
    e. Felicity

Use the following problem to answer questions 21-25:

A group of friends is trying to go to the movie theater to see 3 movies on Saturday. The movie theater is showing six different movies (Movie A – Movie F) that day. They must pick which three they will see based on the following criteria:

- Movies A and C only have one showing and they occur at the same time.
- Movie B can only be watched before Movie C or D, or after Movie F.
- Movies D and F cannot be watched together in any combination.
- Movie E can only be watched if Movie A is watched first or if Movie B is watched second.
- Movie C must be first or second if it is watched.
- Movie D is watched first if Movie A is watched, and it is watched last if Movie C is watched.

21. Which of the following is an acceptable viewing order of the movies?
    a. Movie A, Movie B, Movie F
    b. Movie C, Movie B, Movie E
    c. Movie B, Movie C, Movie D
    d. Movie E, Movie B, Movie C
    e. Movie A, Movie E, Movie D

22. How many different movies could be watched last?
    a. 1
    b. 2
    c. 3
    d. 4
    e. 5

23. If Movie A is watched second, then how many combinations of movies exist?
    a. 0
    b. 1
    c. 2
    d. 3
    e. 4

24. If Movie D is watched last, then which of the following lists all of the movies that could be watched first?
    a. Movies A, B, and E
    b. Movies A and F
    c. Movies C and E
    d. Movies B, C, and E
    e. Movies B, E, and F

25. If Movies B and E are not watched at all, how many permissible combinations of movies exist?
    a. 0
    b. 1
    c. 2
    d. 3
    e. 4

Answer Explanations

1. C: This was a fairly simple question to solve by working through each of the five answer choices to verify their viability with the given rules. Choice *A* is incorrect because Dimitri, Mark, and Aaron are all males, which violates the need to have one male and one female as per the first rule. Choice *B* is not possible because the second rule states that if two females are selected, the male must be Aaron (not Mark). Choice *D* violates the fifth rule. Because Dimitri, Larry, and Clarissa cannot work together in any combination, Clarissa and Larry cannot be on the same team. It also violates the fourth rule, which requires Vanessa to be selected whenever Mark is. Lastly, Clarissa, Aaron, and Mark cannot work together as grouped in Choice *E* because this combination violates the fourth rule that if Mark is selected, Vanessa must also be selected. Choice *C*—Larry, Vanessa, and Mark—is a permissible team because it does not violate any of the rules. The first rule states that at least one male and one female are selected. Vanessa is female and there are two males. The second rule does not apply because there is only one female on the team. Rule 3 is satisfied because Mark is on the team but Aaron is not. Rule 4 is satisfied because Mark and Vanessa are both on the team. Lastly, the fifth rule isn't violated by the team in Choice *C* because, while Mark is on the team, neither Clarissa not Aaron is, so it's a permissible option.

2. B: Using rules 1 and 5 help start the solution process for this problem. Of the six given candidates—Larry, Vanessa, Clarissa, Dimitri, Mark, and Aaron—only two (Vanessa and Clarissa) are female. Rule 1 states that the team must have at least one female, but the fifth rule states that Dimitri cannot be on a team with Clarissa or Larry. This forces the female on Dimitri's team to be Vanessa. That only leaves one open spot, and as per rule 5, it cannot be Larry or Clarissa. The only remaining choices then are Aaron and Mark. Either of these males can take the third spot on the team without violating the rules. Rule 1 is already satisfied. Rule 2 does not apply because only one female is on the team. Rule 3 would not apply because only Aaron *or* Mark could take the third spot since Dimitri and Vanessa already take the other two spots. Rule 4 is satisfied because Vanessa is on the team, so even if Mark is chosen, the rule is not violated, and rule 5 was already addressed. Therefore, there are two possibilities: Dimitri, Vanessa, and Mark; or Dimitri, Vanessa, and Aaron.

3. E: This question can be solved by simply testing the five options and comparing them to the rules. Choices *A* and *D* violate the fifth rule because they place Dimitri or Larry on a team with Clarissa, which is not allowed. Choice *B* violates the second rule because there are two females (Clarissa and Vanessa), but Aaron is not the male on this potential team and he needs to be. Choice *C* is not a viable option because Aaron and Mark cannot be on the same team as per the third rule. The team in Choice *E*—Clarissa, Vanessa, and Aaron—works because it adheres to the second rule (that if two females are chosen, Aaron must be the male) and does not violate any other rules.

4. A: The four males are Dimitri, Larry, Aaron, and Mark, so these are the candidates that can potentially be selected for an all-male team. The third rule states that Aaron and Mark can't work together. The fifth rule states that Dimitri and Larry can't work together. Therefore, it's impossible to get a team of three males together without violating the conditions. For example, if you start with Dimitri, then Mark, Aaron, and Larry remain. Dimitri can't be with Larry, which would force the trio to be Dimitri, Aaron, and Mark, but this violates the third rule. Regardless as to the male you start with, the same two rules will be violated by the different combinations. Therefore, there are no permissible combinations involving only the male employees.

5. E: This was by far the most difficult question of the exercise because it requires all of the combinations to be tested. It is best solved by addressing each applicant individually and determining viable team options that satisfy the given conditions.

Clarissa cannot be with Dimitri or Larry as per rule 5, leaving Vanessa, Aaron, and Mark. As per the second rule, she can be with Vanessa and Aaron together, but not Vanessa and Mark. She can't be with Mark and Aaron together because that would violate the third rule, so that one leaves one option so far: Clarissa, Vanessa, and Aaron.

Larry cannot be with Dimitri or Clarissa per rule 5, leaving Aaron, Mark, and Vanessa. Aaron and Mark cannot be together according to the third rule, so it can't be Larry, Aaron, and Mark. Rule 2 does not apply because only one female of the two (Vanessa) can work with Larry. The fourth rule states that if Mark is chosen, Vanessa must be chosen as well. This means that there are two viable teams for Larry: Larry, Vanessa, and Mark; or Larry, Vanessa, and Aaron. That means, so far, we have three possible teams.

Turning to Dimitri, the fifth rule states that he can't be with Larry or Clarissa, leaving Aaron, Mark, and Vanessa. Again, Aaron and Mark can't be together, so the choices for Dimitri are like those for Larry because those two males have the same conditions applied to them. Therefore, we have two more possible teams: Dimitri, Vanessa, and Mark; or Dimitri, Vanessa, and Aaron, which means there are five viable teams found.

There are no other options not yet addressed for Aaron. Aaron cannot be with Mark as per rule 3. He can be with Vanessa and Clarissa as per rule 2, but this option was already accounted for under Clarissa. Aaron can't be with Clarissa in any other combination besides with Vanessa because only Larry and Dimitri are left and they can't be on the same team with Clarissa in any combination. If Aaron and Vanessa are on the same team, Larry or Dimitri could fill the third spot but these were already accounted for.

Again, Mark can't be with Aaron as per rule 3 and he cannot be with Clarissa as the female as per rule 4. If Mark and Vanessa take two spots and Aaron and Clarissa each can't occupy the third spot, only Larry and Dimitri remain. The trio of Mark, Vanessa, and Larry was accounted for under Larry, while Mark, Vanessa, and Dimitri were accounted for under Dimitri. So, there are no other new options for Mark.

Lastly, Vanessa. According to the second rule, if she's on a team with Clarissa, Aaron must be the male. That was previously accounted for. If she's with Aaron, Mark cannot be the third, leaving Larry or Dimitri. The group containing Dimitri, Vanessa, and Aaron was accounted for under Dimitri. Larry, Vanessa, and Aaron were accounted for under Larry. Therefore, all of the possible combinations have been addressed and there are five total options found.

6. B: The third rule states that Xavier can't be with Thomas or Hector. That leaves Derek, Shaun, or Clayton. However, the fifth rule states that Derek and Xavier can't be together if Derek is picked for point guard. If Xavier is picked for small forward, then Derek will be picked for point guard. That leaves Clayton and Shaun. Either one of these boys could be selected with Xavier without violating any of the rules, making Choice *B* correct. Choices *A, C,* and *D* are all incorrect because they contain Derek, which violates the fifth rule. All choices except Choice *B* violate the third rule because they put Hector on a team that would also contain Xavier.

7. D: Derek would be able to play with Thomas, or he would be able to play with Hector. Note that Hector and Thomas can't play *together,* but each one could individually play with Derek. Derek cannot play with Shaun or Clayton, so Choices *A, B* and *C* are incorrect. Choice *E* is incorrect because if Derek is picked for point guard, he cannot play with Xavier.

8. B: According to the fifth rule, Xavier cannot play small forward if Derek plays guard. According to the fourth rule, when Derek is selected, Clayton and Shaun cannot be. That leaves Hector and Thomas, which is Choice *B*. Hector and Thomas cannot play together, but Hector can play with Derek, and Thomas can play with Derek, as separate pairs.

9. D: This question was solved by simply looking at the rules. Shaun and Derek cannot be on the same team as per the fourth rule. There are no other contradictions with the rules involving Shaun and other players.

10. C: Hector can be with Derek, Shaun, or Clayton. He cannot be with Thomas as per the third rule, so we have three possible pairs.

Derek and Hector are already accounted for and Derek can't be with Shaun or Clayton according to the fourth rule. That leaves Thomas. Derek and Thomas would then be the fourth possible choice.

Thomas cannot be with Hector as per the third rule, and we already counted him with Derek. That leaves Shaun and Clayton. Either player is a viable pair with Thomas, so we have six options.

Shaun was already matched with Hector and Thomas. He cannot be with Derek as per the fourth rule. That leaves Clayton. We now have seven options.

Clayton was already matched with Hector, Thomas, and Shaun, and found to not work with Derek as per the fourth rule. Thus, we have no new pairs, and seven total pairs were found.

11. D: Choices *A* and *B* are not viable options because they don't have Chelsea in between Wade and Jessica, which violates the second rule. Choice *C* places Chelsea on Tuesday, which is not permitted because she is using a blender, and rule three states that blenders cannot be used on Tuesday. Choice *D* is a permissible order. It has Victor after Jessica, which satisfies the first rule. It has Chelsea in between Jessica and Wade, adhering to the second rule. Victor is not using blender and he is on Tuesday, which works with the third rule. Lastly, it has Riley on Wednesday, which abides by the fourth rule. Therefore, no rules are violated. Choice *E* is not possible because it violates the first rule, which states that Victor must bring his snack after Jessica.

12. E: There are five students: Jessica, Wade, Victor, Chelsea, and Riley. Jessica cannot bring the class snack on Friday because according to the first rule, Victor has to provide snack after her and there are no school days after Friday. This eliminates Choices *B*, *C*, and *D*. Chelsea cannot go on Friday because the second rule places her somewhere between Wade and Jessica. This eliminates Choice *A*, leaving just Choice *E*. However, let's run through the other options. Riley cannot go on Friday because the fourth rule forces him to go on Tuesday or Wednesday. That leaves Victor and Wade, either of whom can go on Friday without violating any of the rules.

13. E: If Victor is on Wednesday, Riley must be on Tuesday because of the fourth rule. That means that Jessica must bring snacks on Monday so that Victor comes after her. That means that Chelsea would be on Thursday and Wade on Friday to keep Chelsea in between Jessica and Wade, as stated in the second rule.

14. D: Option 1 is Wade, Chelsea, Riley, Jessica, Victor. This combination works because Victor is bringing snacks after Jessica, which satisfies rule 1. Chelsea is between Wade and Jessica, which satisfies rule 2. Since blenders must be used on Tuesday, this satisfies the new rule. Riley is on Wednesday, which satisfies rule 4.

Option 2 is Jessica, Chelsea, Riley, Wade, and Victor. This combination works because Victor is bringing snacks after Jessica, which satisfies rule 1. Chelsea is between Wade and Jessica, which satisfies rule 2. Chelsea is on Tuesday, which satisfies the new rule—that blenders must be used on Tuesday. Riley is bringing snacks on Wednesday, which satisfies the fourth rule.

Option 3 is Jessica, Chelsea, Riley, Victor, and Wade. This combination works because Victor is bringing snacks after Jessica, which satisfies the first rule. Chelsea is between Jessica and Wade, which satisfies the second rule. Chelsea is on Tuesday, which satisfies the new rule about blenders being used on Tuesday. Riley is on Wednesday, which satisfies the fourth rule.

15. B: If Wade is out of town Monday, he cannot bring the snack on Monday. We already determined that he cannot go on Tuesday because he is using a blender. If Wade were to bring snacks on Wednesday, Riley would be on Tuesday. Again, this won't work because Chelsea needs to be between Wade and Jessica, pushing her to Thursday, Jessica to Friday, which again leaves no room for Victor. If Wade was on Thursday, Jessica could be Monday, Chelsea on Tuesday (to keep her in between Wade and Jessica), Riley on Wednesday (as per the fourth rule), and Victor on Friday, which still satisfies the first rule. Lastly, if Wade was Friday, Jessica could bring snacks on Monday, Riley could bring snacks on Tuesday, Chelsea on Wednesday, and Victor on Thursday. Or, we could have Jessica, Victor, Riley, Chelsea, then Wade.

16. C: For this question, it makes sense to run through each of the choices to see if they violate one of the five given rules. As soon as it is determined that at least one rule is violated by the order provided in the answer choice, that answer can be eliminated, and the rest of the rules do not need to be checked. Choice *C* does not violate any of the rules, so it is correct. The third rule is violated by Choice *A* because Duane is assigned to the second time slot and Greg is assigned to the fourth, so *A* cannot be correct. Duane must present after Greg. Choice *B* violates the fifth rule because Brenda and Duane are not presenting back-to-back, so Choice *B* is wrong. Choice *D* violates the first rule since Jackie is fifth and Harold is sixth, so *D* cannot be correct. Lastly, Choice *E* violates the fourth rule because neither Greg nor Felicity is in the fourth slot, so Choice *E* is incorrect.

17. E: Some test takers may feel most comfortable solving this problem using diagramming and drawing the seven slots and placing Brenda in the third slot. Duane cannot be fourth because the fourth rule states that either Greg or Felicity is fourth. This means that according to the fifth rule, Duane must be second, because Duane and Brenda present consecutively. Because Duane is in the second time slot, Greg must be first because the third rule states that Duane has to present later than Greg. Placing Greg in the first time slot allows us to confidently put Felicity in fourth, since Felicity or Greg has to be fourth (according to the fourth rule), and Greg is already first. Since Harold and Jackie cannot be in consecutive slots without violating the first rule, one of them must be in slot five and the other in slot seven, which means that Carlos is in slot six, separating them. The answer choice has been found; Carlos must be in the sixth slot, making Choice *E* correct. We cannot definitively determine which slot Harold and Jackie each occupy with the given information. Theoretically, Jackie *could* be in the seventh slot (Choice *A*), but the question is looking for a placement that *must* be true and we don't know her position for sure, making this an incorrect answer. The other answer choices place a student in the incorrect slot.

18. B: Solving this question requires combining rules 2, 3, and 5. Brenda cannot present first because Brenda and Duane must be consecutive (rule 5) and the third rule states that Duane must present later than Greg. If Brenda was first (Choice *A*), Duane would have to be next after her in slot two, but this would violate rule 3, since Greg did not present in the lineup before Duane.

Duane could be in the fifth slot if Barbara was in the sixth and Jackie in the seventh, so Choice *B* is possible.

Harold cannot present sixth because if he did, Brenda and Duane would need to be in second and third with Greg in first, because Brenda and Duane need to be consecutive and with Carlos in third and Felicity or Greg only allowed in fourth, there would not be any other consecutive spots. Duane has to go sometime after Greg, so Greg would be first. This would leave no viable time slots for Jackie since according to the first rule, Jackie and Harold cannot be consecutive. If Harold is sixth, the only open spots for Jackie are next to him. Therefore, Choice C cannot be possible.

Greg cannot present seventh because Brenda, Duane, and Jackie must all go after him. Therefore, Choice D is incorrect.

Choice E lists an invalid placement as well. Jackie cannot present third, since Brenda, Duane, and Greg all need to go before her.

19. E: Again, this problem may be solved most easily by diagramming the seven slots. Carlos must be put in the third slot first. This forces Brenda and Duane to occupy slots five and six (in either order) because Duane needs to be after Greg. With Carlos in third and either Felicity or Greg in fourth, Brenda and Duane can't be in third or fourth. They cannot go first and second because Duane needs to be sometime after Greg. With Duane and Brenda in slots five and six, Jackie is forced into the seventh presentation slot since according to rule 2, she needs to be sometime after Brenda. Therefore, Choice E is impossible. All of the other choices are viable. As mentioned, Brenda and Duane can be in fifth and sixth (either person in either spot). Felicity can be in fourth, pushing Greg to first or second, which is fine because he'd still be before Duane. Harold would need to be in whichever space (first or second) that Greg did not occupy in order to separate him from Jackie and satisfy the first rule. As such, he can also go first, making Choice D possible as well.

20. D: If Harold is in the seventh time slot, Felicity must be fourth instead of Greg. This is because if Greg was in the fourth spot, there would be an inadequate number of slots for Brenda, Duane, and Jackie after him but before Harold. (Remember that Duane and Brenda must be consecutive, Duane must be sometime after Greg, and Jackie sometime after Brenda.) With Felicity in the fourth slot, only the second and third slots are permissible for Brenda and Duane, which would force Greg into the first slot so that he precedes Duane (as per rule 3). Jackie cannot be next to Harold without violating the first rule, but she must be sometime after Brenda. Therefore, she has to be in the fifth time slot since Harold is seventh (so she can't be sixth), and Carlos would present in the sixth spot to split up Harold and Jackie. Since Jackie is in the fifth spot, Choice D is correct.

21. C: Choice A is invalid because it violates the second rule by having Movie B before, not after, Movie F. Choice B does not work because according to the second rule, Movie B can only be watched before Movie C or D, or after Movie F. Here it is after, not before, Movie C. Choice C is possible because it does not violate any rules. It adheres to the second rule by having Movie B before Movie C. It has Movie D but not Movie F, so the third rule is followed. Movie E is not in the lineup, so the fourth rule doesn't apply. Movie C is second, so it abides by the fifth rule. Lastly, it follows the sixth rule because Movie D is last because Movie C is watched. Choice D has Movie C third, which contradicts the fifth rule. Choice E cannot work because it violates the last rule, which states that if Movie A and D are both watched, Movie D must be first, but it is third here.

22. E: There are six movies. We know that Movie C must be first or second if it is watched, so it cannot be last. Any of the other movies can theoretically be last, depending on the other two in the lineup.

23. B: It makes sense to address this question rule by rule to determine viable lineups. According to the first rule, Movies A and C cannot be played together, so we know that Movie C is not one of the choices.

Movie E cannot be in the lineup when Movie A is second because it would violate the fourth rule. Per the sixth rule, if Movie A is watched, Movie D is first. That would mean Movie D is first and A is second. This means Movie B cannot be third since it needs to be before D or C or after Movie F per the second rule. We already ruled out Movies C and E from the lineup, so Movie D cannot go first when Movie A is in second. It also cannot go third because of the same rule, so now we know Movies C, D, and E cannot be in the lineup. That leaves Movies B and F. Per the second rule, Movie B must be seen after Movie F, so a permissible order would be Movie F, Movie A, and then Movie B.

24. D: The third rule states the Movies D and F cannot be played together, so Choices *B* and *E* are incorrect. Choice *A* is incorrect because it includes Movie A in the first slot, but according to the sixth rule, Movie D must be first, not last, if Movie A is played. Movie C can be shown first and D last without violating any rules, but then there would be just permissible movie in second (B), since A cannot be shown with C and F cannot be shown with D. That only leaves Movie B and Movie E for the second spot. Movie E cannot be in the second spot without A in first per the third rule. Movie B can be second per the second rule because even though it is after C, it is before Movie D and it must before C *or* D, but not necessarily both. Movie B can be watched first when D is last if C is second. Lastly, because of the fourth rule, Movie E can be first when D is last as long as Movie B is in second, which we just found is possible.

25. A: If Movies B and E are not watched, we are left with Movies A, C, D, and F. Movies A and C cannot be shown consecutively according to the first rule, which means each would need to be shown with D and F. However, D and F cannot be combined together, which means that no viable lineups exist.

Reading Comprehension

Topic, Main Idea, and Supporting Details

The *topic* of a text is the general subject matter. Text topics can usually be expressed in one word, or a few words at most. Additionally, readers should ask themselves what point the author is trying to make. This point is the *main idea* or *primary purpose* of the text, the principal thing the author wants readers to know concerning the topic. Once the author has established the main idea, he or she will support the main idea by supporting details. Supporting details are evidence that support the main idea and include personal testimonies, examples, or statistics.

One analogy for these components and their relationships is that a text is like a well-designed house. The topic is the roof, covering all rooms. The main idea is the frame. The supporting details are the various rooms. To identify the topic of a text, readers can ask themselves what or who the author is writing about in the paragraph. To locate the main idea, readers can ask themselves what one idea the author wants readers to know about the topic. To identify supporting details, readers can put the main idea into question form and ask, "what does the author use to prove or explain their main idea?"

Let's look at an example. An author is writing an essay about the Amazon rainforest and trying to convince the audience that more funding should go into protecting the area from deforestation. The author makes the argument stronger by including evidence of the benefits of the rainforest: it provides habitats to a variety of species, it provides much of the earth's oxygen which in turn cleans the atmosphere, and it is the home to medicinal plants that may be the answer to some of the world's deadliest diseases. Here is an outline of the essay looking at topic, main idea, and supporting details:

- Topic: Amazon rainforest
- Main Idea: The Amazon rainforest should receive more funding to protect it from deforestation.
- Supporting Details:
  - 1. It provides habitats to a variety of species.
  - 2. It provides much of the earth's oxygen, which, in turn, cleans the atmosphere.
  - 3. It is home to medicinal plants that may treat some of the world's deadliest diseases.

Notice that the topic of the essay is listed in a few key words: "Amazon rainforest." The main idea tells us what about the topic is important: that the topic should be funded in order to prevent deforestation. Finally, the supporting details are what author relies on to convince the audience to act or to believe in the truth of the main idea.

Information that is Explicitly Stated

In the Reading Comprehension section of the LSAT, test takers will be asked questions based on their direct knowledge of the passage. The information explicitly stated in the passage leaves the reader no room for confusion. The sections below allow test takers to determine what type of information is explicitly stated in the passage. Readers should consider the following questions when reviewing a passage: Is the information an author's opinion or an objective fact? Does the information contain bias or stereotype? And within the information stated, what words are directly stated and what words leave room for a connotative interpretation?

Being cautious of the author's presentation of information will aid the test taker in determining the correct answer choice for the question stem.

Facts and Opinions

A fact is a statement that is true empirically or an event that has actually occurred in reality, and can be proven or supported by evidence; it is generally objective. In contrast, an opinion is subjective, representing something that someone believes rather than something that exists in the absolute. People's individual understandings, feelings, and perspectives contribute to variations in opinion. Although facts are typically objective in nature, in some instances, a statement of fact may be both factual and yet also subjective. For example, emotions are individual subjective experiences. If an individual says that they feel happy or sad, the feeling is subjective, but the statement is factual; hence, it is a subjective fact. In contrast, if one person tells another that the other is feeling happy or sad—whether this is true or not—that is an assumption or an opinion.

Biases

Biases usually occur when someone allows their personal preferences or ideologies to interfere with what should be an objective decision. In personal situations, someone is biased towards someone if they favor them in an unfair way. In academic writing, being biased in your sources means leaving out objective information that would turn the argument one way or the other. The evidence of bias in academic writing makes the text less credible, so be sure to present all viewpoints when writing, not just your own, so to avoid coming off as biased. Being objective when presenting information or dealing with people usually allows the author to gain more credibility.

Stereotypes

Stereotypes are preconceived notions that place a particular rule or characteristics on an entire group of people. Stereotypes are usually offensive to the group they refer to or to allies of that group, and often have negative connotations. The reinforcement of stereotypes isn't always obvious. Sometimes stereotypes can be very subtle and are still widely used in order for people to understand categories within the world. For example, saying that women are more intuitive or nurturing than men is a stereotype, although this is still an assumption used by many in order to understand differences between one another.

Denotation and Connotation

Denotation refers to a word's explicit definition, like that found in the dictionary. Denotation is often set in comparison to connotation. Connotation is the emotional, cultural, social, or personal implication associated with a word. Denotation is more of an objective definition, whereas connotation can be more subjective, although many connotative meanings of words are similar for certain cultures. The denotative meanings of words are usually based on facts, and the connotative meanings of words are usually based on emotion.

Here are some examples of words and their denotative and connotative meanings in Western culture:

Word	Denotative Meaning	Connotative Meaning
Home	A permanent place where one lives, usually as a member of a family.	A place of warmth; a place of familiarity; comforting; a place of safety and security. "Home" usually has a positive connotation.
Snake	A long reptile with no limbs and strong jaws that moves along the ground; some snakes have a poisonous bite.	An evil omen; a slithery creature (human or nonhuman) that is deceitful or unwelcome. "Snake" usually has a negative connotation.
Winter	A season of the year that is the coldest, usually from December to February in the northern hemisphere and from June to August in the southern hemisphere.	Circle of life, especially that of death and dying; cold or icy; dark and gloomy; hibernation, sleep, or rest. Winter can have a negative connotation, although many who have access to heat may enjoy the snowy season from their homes.

Information or Ideas that can be Inferred

One technique authors often use to make their fictional stories more interesting is not giving away too much information by providing hints and descriptions. It is then up to the reader to draw a conclusion about the author's meaning by connecting textual clues with the reader's own pre-existing experiences and knowledge. Drawing conclusions is important as a reading strategy for understanding what is occurring in a text. Rather than directly stating who, what, where, when, or why, authors often describe story elements. Then, readers must draw conclusions to understand significant story components. As they go through a text, readers can think about the setting, characters, plot, problem, and solution; whether the author provided any clues for consideration; and combine any story clues with their existing knowledge and experiences to draw conclusions about what occurs in the text.

Making Predictions

Before and during reading, readers can apply the strategy of making predictions about what they think may happen next. For example, what plot and character developments will occur in fiction? What points will the author discuss in nonfiction? Making predictions about portions of text they have not yet read prepares readers mentally, and also gives them a purpose for reading. To inform and make predictions about text, the reader can do the following:

- Consider the title of the text and what it implies
- Look at the cover of the book
- Look at any illustrations or diagrams for additional visual information
- Analyze the structure of the text
- Apply outside experience and knowledge to the text

Readers may adjust their predictions as they read. Reader predictions may or may not come true in text.

Making Inferences

Authors describe settings, characters, characters' emotions, and events. Readers must infer to understand the text fully. Inferring enables readers to figure out meanings of unfamiliar words, make predictions about upcoming text, draw conclusions, and reflect on reading. Readers can infer about text before, during, and after reading. In everyday life, we use sensory information to infer. Readers can do the same with text. When authors do not answer all reader questions, readers must infer by looking at illustrations, considering characters' behaviors, and asking questions during reading. Taking clues from text and connecting text to prior knowledge help to draw conclusions. Readers can infer word meanings, settings, reasons for occurrences, character emotions, pronoun referents, author messages, and answers to questions unstated in text.

Making inferences and drawing conclusions involve skills that are quite similar: both require readers to fill in information the author has omitted. Authors may omit information as a technique for inducing readers to discover the outcomes themselves; or they may consider certain information unimportant; or they may assume their reading audience already knows certain information. To make an inference or draw a conclusion about text, readers should observe all facts and arguments the author has presented and consider what they already know from their own personal experiences. Reading students taking multiple-choice tests that refer to text passages can determine correct and incorrect choices based on the information in the passage. For example, from a text passage describing an individual's signs of anxiety while unloading groceries and nervously clutching their wallet at a grocery store checkout, readers can infer or conclude that the individual may not have enough money to pay for everything.

The Purpose of Words or Phrases as Used in Context

Readers can often figure out what unfamiliar words mean without interrupting their reading to look them up in dictionaries by examining context. Context includes the other words or sentences in a passage. One common context clue is the root word and any affixes (prefixes/suffixes). Another common context clue is a synonym or definition included in the sentence. Sometimes both exist in the same sentence. Here's an example:

Scientists who study birds are *ornithologists*.

Many readers may not know the word *ornithologist*. However, the example contains a definition (scientists who study birds). The reader may also have the ability to analyze the suffix (*-logy*, meaning the study of) and root (*ornitho-*, meaning bird).

Another common context clue is a sentence that shows differences. Here's an example:

Birds *incubate* their eggs outside of their bodies, unlike mammals.

Some readers may be unfamiliar with the word *incubate*. However, since we know that "unlike mammals," birds incubate their eggs outside of their bodies, we can infer that *incubate* has something to do with keeping eggs warm outside the body until they are hatched.

In addition to analyzing the etymology of a word's root and affixes and extrapolating word meaning from sentences that contrast an unknown word with an antonym, readers can also determine word meanings from sentence context clues based on logic. Here's an example:

Birds are always looking out for *predators* that could attack their young.

The reader who is unfamiliar with the word *predator* could determine from the context of the sentence that predators usually prey upon baby birds and possibly other young animals. Readers might also use the context clue of etymology here, as *predator* and *prey* have the same root.

When readers encounter an unfamiliar word in text, they can use the surrounding context—the overall subject matter, specific chapter/section topic, and especially the immediate sentence context. Among others, one category of context clues is grammar. For example, the position of a word in a sentence and its relationship to the other words can help the reader establish whether the unfamiliar word is a verb, a noun, an adjective, an adverb, etc. This narrows down the possible meanings of the word to one part of speech. However, this may be insufficient. In a sentence that many birds *migrate* twice yearly, the reader can determine the word is a verb, and that probably does not mean eat or drink; but it could mean travel, mate, lay eggs, hatch, or molt.

Some words can have a number of different meanings depending on how they are used. For example, the word *fly* has a different meaning in each of the following sentences:

- "His trousers have a fly on them."
- "He swatted the fly on his trousers."
- "Those are some fly trousers."
- "They went fly fishing."
- "She hates to fly."
- "If humans were meant to fly, they would have wings."

As strategies, readers can try substituting a familiar word for an unfamiliar one and see whether it makes sense in the sentence. They can also identify other words in a sentence, offering clues to an unfamiliar word's meaning.

The Organization or Structure

Text structure is the way in which the author organizes and presents textual information so readers can follow and comprehend it. One kind of text structure is sequence. This means the author arranges the text in a logical order from beginning to middle to end. There are three types of sequences:

- Chronological: ordering events in time from earliest to latest

- Spatial: describing objects, people, or spaces according to their relationships to one another in space

- Order of Importance: addressing topics, characters, or ideas according to how important they are, from either least important to most important or most important to least importance

Chronological sequence is the most common sequential text structure. Readers can identify sequential structure by looking for words that signal it, like *first, earlier, meanwhile, next, then, later, finally,* or the inclusion of specific times and dates the author includes as chronological references.

Problem-Solution Text Structure
The problem-solution text structure organizes textual information by presenting readers with a problem and then developing its solution throughout the course of the text. The author may present a variety of alternatives as possible solutions, eliminating each as they are found unsuccessful, or gradually leading up to the ultimate solution. For example, in fiction, an author might write a murder mystery novel and have the character(s) solve it through investigating various clues or character alibis until the killer is identified.

In nonfiction, an author writing an essay or book on a real-world problem might discuss various alternatives and explain their disadvantages or why they would not work before identifying the best solution. For scientific research, an author reporting and discussing scientific experiment results would explain why various alternatives failed or succeeded.

Comparison-Contrast Text Structure

Comparison identifies similarities between two or more things. *Contrast* identifies differences between two or more things. Authors typically employ both to illustrate relationships between things by highlighting their commonalities and deviations. For example, a writer might compare Windows and Linux as operating systems, and contrast Linux as free and open-source vs. Windows as proprietary. When writing an essay, sometimes it is useful to create an image of the two objects or events you are comparing or contrasting. Venn diagrams are useful because they show the differences as well as the similarities between two things. Once you've seen the similarities and differences on paper, it might be helpful to create an outline of the essay with both comparison and contrast. Every outline will look different, because every two or more things will have a different number of comparisons and contrasts. Say you are trying to compare and contrast carrots with sweet potatoes. Here is an example of a compare/contrast outline using those topics:

- Introduction: State why you are comparing and contrasting the foods. Give the thesis statement.
- Body paragraph 1: Sweet potatoes and carrots are both root vegetables (similarity)
- Body paragraph 2: Sweet potatoes and carrots are both orange (similarity)
- Body paragraph 3: Sweet potatoes and carrots have different nutritional profiles (difference)
- Conclusion: Restate the purpose and key points of your comparison/contrast essay.

Of course, if there is only one similarity between your topics and two differences, you will want to rearrange your outline. Always tailor your essay to what works best with your topic.

Descriptive Text Structure

Description can be both a type of text structure and a type of text. Some texts are descriptive throughout entire books. For example, a book may describe the geography of a certain country, state, or region, or tell readers all about dolphins by describing their various characteristics. Many other texts are not descriptive throughout, but use descriptive passages within the overall text. The following are a few examples of descriptive texts:

- When the author describes a character in a novel
- When the author sets the scene for an event by describing the setting.
- When a biographer describes the personality and behaviors of a real-life individual
- When a historian describes the details of a particular battle within a book about a specific war
- When a travel writer describes the climate, people, foods, and/or customs of a certain place

A hallmark of description is using sensory details, painting a vivid picture so readers can imagine it almost as if they were experiencing it personally.

Cause and Effect Text Structure

When using cause and effect to extrapolate meaning from text, readers must determine the cause when the author only communicates effects. For example, if a description of a child eating an ice cream cone includes details like beads of sweat forming on the child's face and the ice cream dripping down her hand faster than she can lick it off, the reader can infer or conclude it must be hot outside. A useful technique for making such decisions is wording them in "If/then" form, like the following: "If the child is perspiring and the ice cream melting, it must be a hot day." Cause and effect text structures explain why certain events or actions resulted in particular outcomes. For example, to explain how the dodo was hunted into extinction, an author might describe America's historical large flocks of dodo birds, the fact that gunshots did not startle/frighten dodos, and that because dodos did not flee, settlers killed whole flocks in one hunting session.

The Application of Information in the Selection to a New Context

There will be questions on the LSAT that give a scenario with a general conclusion and ask you to apply that general conclusion to a new context. Skills for making inferences and drawing conclusions will be helpful in the first portion of this question. Reading the initial scenario carefully and finding the general concept, or the bigger picture, is necessary for when the test taker attempts to apply this general concept to the new context the question provides. Here is an example of a test question that asks the test taker to apply information in a selection to a new context:

The placebo effect is a phenomenon used in clinical trial studies to test the effectiveness of new medications. A group of people are given either the new medication or the placebo, but are not told which they receive. Interestingly, about one-third of people who are given the placebo in clinical trials will report a cessation of their symptoms. In one trial in 1925, a group of people were given sugar pills and told their migraines should dissipate as a result of the pills. Forty-two percent noticed that in the following six months, their weekly migraines evaporated. Researchers believe that human belief and expectation might be a reason that the placebo will work in some patients.

Considering the phenomenon of the placebo effect, what would probably happen to someone who is given a shot with no medication and told their arm should go numb from it?

    a. The patient might experience some burning in their arm, but then they would feel nothing.
    b. The patient would feel their arm going numb, as the placebo effect is certain to work.
    c. Nothing would happen, because the shot does not actually have any medication in it.
    d. The individual might actually experience a numbing sensation in their arm, as the placebo works on some people by simply being told the placebo will have certain effects.
    e. The patient's arm will hurt more than normal because the placebo effect will increase their discomfort.

The answer is Choice *D*. The individual might actually experience a numbing sensation in their arm, as the placebo works on some people by simply being told the placebo will have certain effects. Choices *B* and *C* are too absolute to be considered correct—watch out for words like "never" or "always" in the answer choices so you can rule them out if possible. Choice *A* is incorrect because we don't know what the initial sensation of the shot would feel like for this individual. The placebo effect would have a chance of working with the shot, just like it would have a chance of working in the above example with the pill. The patient's belief in an effect is what can possibly manifest the desired result of the placebo. Choice *E* is incorrect. Although there's no medication in the injection so the arm may hurt, this would be the opposite of the placebo effect.

Principles that Function in the Selection

In the LSAT Reading Comprehension section, there will be several questions that ask the test taker about principles expressed in the selection. A principle functions as a fundamental truth used as a basis for a scenario or system of reasoning. Principles are able to function in three ways: (1) principles as the cause of something or as a final cause; (2) principles as moral, juridical, or scientific law; and (3) principles as axiom or self-evident truths.

Principles as Cause

Principles can function in different ways according to the way we express the principle. For the circumstance of cause and effect, principle refers to the cause that was efficient for the effect to come into existence. The principle as cause is traced back to Aristotelian reasoning, which surmises that every event is moved by something prior to it, or has a cause.

Principles as Law

We see principles as law at work in moral law, juridical law, and scientific law. In moral law, principles are what our predecessors teach us as children. "Do unto others," or the "golden rule," is a principle that society has embedded in us so that we are able to function as a civilized people. Principles as moral law are restrictive to the individual as a way of protecting the other person, the whole, or society.

Principles in juridical law are created by the State and also function to limit the liberty of individuals in order to protect the masses. The principles formed in juridical law are written rules that seek to establish a foundation which people can adhere to. The "homestead principle" is an example of a principle in juridical law. The "homestead principle" would function as someone gaining ownership of land because they have made it into a farm, or utilized some resource that has been unused on the land prior to their cultivation of it.

Principles as scientific law function as natural laws, including the Laws of Thermodynamics or natural selection. Principles in scientific law function as laws used to predict certain phenomena that happen in nature. In this context, principles are able to predict results of future experiments. They are developed from facts and also have the ability to be strongly supported by observational evidence.

Principles as Axioms

The LSAT may also ask questions based on principles as axioms, which are statements that are given to be true or serve as a premise for something. It is important to remember that the world of the question is absolute. That is, the foundation of the passage should be unquestioned by the test taker—the principles in the passage are considered absolutely true, no matter if they seem strange. The following list includes tips and sample questions that may be asked in the principle questions:

- What is the principle expressed in the passage?
- How does the stated principle impact the passage?
- The reasoning in the passage most conforms to which of the following principles?
- Which one of the following principles, if valid, most helps to justify the reasoning in the passage?

Some questions may include two passages, where one states the principle and the other applies it. The following is an example of the type of logical thinking you will need for principle questions on the LSAT:

A mountain climbing crew is headed up Mount Everest. The leader of the crew is a man in his sixties. His son is on the crew, with ten other individuals whom he has just met. They are all tied together with a rope. A powerful avalanche occurs, and the leader's son is knocked off a portion of the cliff and is pulling the rest of the crew down with him. It is apparent to the entire crew that if they remain tied to the son, they will all die. The leader is the only man with a knife available. He takes the knife out, tells his son he loves him, and cuts the rope.

The leader's reasoning in the passage most conforms to which of the following principles?

   a. The principle that an action is just if it benefits the majority.
   b. The principle that an action is just if it benefits those you love.
   c. The principle that certain actions are ethically right if they maximize one's own interest.
   d. The principle that a consequence should be equal to the action in question.
   e. The principle that blood is thicker than water.

For principle questions, take each answer choice and make it absolutely true in the world of the passage. Let's look at Choice *B*. In the world of the passage, if the leader held this principle to be true, what would he have done? He probably would have done anything to save his son, even if it meant risking his own life and the life of the crew. This choice is incorrect. The same reasoning applies to Choice *E* because the saying that "blood is thicker than water" means that family ties are more important and stronger than all others. Choice *C* is also incorrect, although this might be a difficult moral question to answer. Was the leader acting in his own interest? His own life was saved in the process of letting his son go, so it can be argued this was the case. However, the flipside to this dilemma is that for the rest of his life, the leader would have to live with the death of his son, and so his best interest may have been to risk the crew's life to save his son. This would, in the long run, serve to alleviate his feelings of guilt. This principle is not the best principle to apply to the passage. Choice *D* is incorrect. This principle would apply to the leader *after the incident* when he must own up to the consequences of his actions, but it does not apply to the current situation in the passage.

Choice *A* is the correct answer choice. We see that the leader chooses to act in the best interest of the majority. He lets his son go so that the rest of the crew (the majority) does not fall off the cliff. Ultimately, this is the principle of utilitarianism, which states that an action is right if it benefits the majority. In the world of the passage, the leader is in accordance with this principle based on his actions.

Here's another example of picking out a principle that applies to the selection:

Julie is staying with her grandmother for Thanksgiving. Julie and her grandmother have disagreed many times during the vacation because Julie politely declines to eat the meals her grandmother cooks if they have meat in them. Julie also does not like participating in the cattle roping her family does for fun on the weekends. Julie's grandmother wants Julie to be part of the culture and fit in with everyone else, so Julie takes up knitting so that she can relate to her grandmother in a way that speaks to her culture.

Julie's reasoning in the passage most conforms to which of the following principles?

   a. Respect your elders and learn by their wisdom.
   b. Everything happens for a reason.
   c. Never harm, or participate in the harming of, a living thing.
   d. All animals have souls and should be treated as humans.
   e. A stitch in time can save nine.

Choice *A* is incorrect. The choice states to respect your elders and learn by their wisdom. Julie does attempt to respect her grandmother by learning how to knit. However, Julie would in fact sacrifice her principle (do no harm) if she were to abide by the wisdom of her elders. Julie is not trying to conform to this principle with her reasoning. Choice *B* is also incorrect. We don't see an argument about purpose or a reason for cause happening, so we can mark this one off. Choice *D* is also incorrect—all animals have souls and should be treated as humans. This one is tricky because we see Julie abstaining from participating in eating meat and from joining in certain activities with them. This one is tempting, but

Choice *C* is a much clearer, broader principle we can apply to Julie's line of thinking. Choice *E* is also incorrect. Although the tie-in to knitting may be tempting, the idiom "a stitch in time saves nine" means that taking the time to right a problem immediately will save much more time and work in the long run.

Choice *C* states to never harm, or participate in the harming of, a living thing. We can tell that Julie's line of thinking conforms best with this principle. Once accepted, principles will direct a person to live one way or another. Julie has accepted not only to not harm a living thing, but to not participate in the harming of a living thing. We can see this by her refusal to eat what her grandmother prepares as well as her refusal to participate in the cattle roping. We also see Julie attempting to repair the hurt feelings between her and her grandmother.

Analogies to Claims or Arguments in the Selection

In its most basic form, an analogy compares two different things. For the LSAT, an analogy question is a situation that parallels the principles or foundations given in another situation. The source, or analogue, will require you to pick out the most apt target in a set of particular events. Analogy questions are different from principle questions in that they work with two particular situations, instead of working with applying a general principle to a particular situation. In law school, students may find that many cases are determined by precedent case law, where an analogy will be drawn based on facts from a prior case to determine the outcome of a current case.

Analogy questions in the LSAT look like the following:

Based on the hypothetical situation given in paragraph 4, which of the following is most closely analogous?

The answer choices will consist of five particular situations that attempt to mirror the hypothetical situation given in the passage. In order to find the correct answer, it might be helpful to know the basics of what an analogy is.

The following is a list of different types of analogies:

Category	Example
Part to whole	"All screwdrivers are considered tools."
	Tools is the whole, and screwdrivers is the part to that whole. Be careful of reversing this logic, though. It would be an error to say "Likewise, all tools are considered screwdrivers." In simplified terms, saying "All A are B" is not the same as saying "All B are A."
Confusing causation with correlation	"The number of traffic accidents in Florida has gone up this past summer. The temperature has also increased this summer by 10 degrees. I bet the heat is making drivers more irritable." This logic confuses causation (the heat is causing accidents) with correlation. Traffic accidents have gone up and so has the heat, but that doesn't necessarily mean that one is causing the other. A new smartphone could have been released, creating distracted drivers. Or, there could have been more rain in the summer, causing dangerous driving conditions.

Category	Example
Performer to related action	"A lawyer passes the bar exam after finishing law school." "A student passes the SAT after finishing high school." Performer to related action requires a test taker to make an association between actions and their performers. Here, we see a performer passing some kind of exam after they've gone through years of training. In this way, the student and their actions are analogous to the lawyer and their actions.
Cause and effect	"A restaurant was shut down because it had an infestation problem." "A company went out of business because it couldn't produce enough inventory." In the analogy above, we see something shutting down because of a problem. The cause and effect analogy presents an unequivocal effect to an action and requires no effort to make something happen.
Unintended consequence	"Two parents enter therapy with the purpose of finding help for their son, who is struggling with substance abuse and behavioral problems at school. As a result, they find that they also are dealing with unresolved issues in the past and learn ways to cope with these issues." Here, a group of people set out to do one thing, and receive another in return. In this situation, there is an unintended consequence beside an intended consequence. In some situations, the intended consequence might not happen at all, and the unintended consequence will have the opposite effect of the intended consequence, creating an ironic situation.

Let's look at an example of an analogy question on the LSAT Reading Comprehension section. It is a passage from *Ten Great Events in History* by James Johonnot:

Meantime, in the Church of England a spirit of criticism had grown up. Stricter thinkers disliked the imposing ceremonies which the English church still retained: some of the ministers ceased to wear gowns in preaching, performed the marriage ceremony without using a ring, and were in favor of simplifying all the church service. Unpretentious workers began to tire of the everlasting quarreling, and to long for a religion simple and quiet. These soon met trouble, for the rulers had decided that salvation was by the Church of England, as the sovereign, its head, should order. Dissent was the two-fold guilt of heresy and revolution—sin against God and crime against the king and English law. They were forbidden to preach at all if they would not wear a gown during service, and the people who went to hear them were punished. This treatment caused serious thought among the "non-conformists," as they were called, and, once thinking, they soon concluded that the king had no such supreme right to order the church, and the church had over its ministers no such right of absolute dictation.

Given Johonnot's account of the criticism of the Church of England in the Middle Ages, which one of the following is most analogous to the situation of the ministers' refusal to wear gowns and the workers' resistance of fighting leading to problems with the church?

   a. A church body meets resistance from an outside secular entity for issues related to social injustice.
   b. Three members of a sorority refuse to do the hazing ritual, so they are kicked out of the sorority by the other members.
   c. A group of kids at school who create an exclusive club that says anyone can join as long as they are in second grade and live on Magnolia Street.
   d. A book club that finds it is no longer useful to its members, and thus attempts to change the group to a film club instead.
   e. An elephant who is sick and cannot make the journey with its tribe finds it is being held up by the rest of the members of the group so that it can walk the rest of the way.

What we have in the original source are members part of a group refusing to participate in a tradition, so as a result, they are punished by the group. The ministers and workers are refusing to participate in church traditions, so they are punished or banished by the church.

Choice *B* is the correct answer to this analogy question. We have members of a group refusing to participate in a tradition (a hazing ritual), so they are punished by the other members of the group. This target most closely fits the original analogy.

Choice *A* is incorrect. Although we are dealing with a church, the structure of the analogy is not the same. In this situation, the group is experiencing external problems rather than internal problems depicted in the original source.

Choice *C* is incorrect because this analogy depicts a creation of a group and the rules for joining. In the original analogy, the group is already established with its laws and traditions.

Choice *D* is incorrect because this group is able to adapt to dissent as a whole, and is not in disagreement about traditions that are no longer working.

Finally, Choice *E* is incorrect. The group in question is supporting and helping a member who is sick. In the original source, the members aren't sick, but in disagreement, and they certainly aren't being supported.

An Author's Attitude as Revealed in the Tone of a Passage or the Language Used

Some question stems in the LSAT Reading Comprehension section will ask about the author's attitude toward a certain person or idea. While it may seem impossible to know exactly what the author felt toward their subject, there are clues to indicate the emotion, or lack thereof, of the author. Clues like word choice or style will alert readers to the author's attitude. Some possible words that name the author's attitude are listed below:

- Admiring
- Angry
- Critical
- Defensive
- Enthusiastic
- Humorous
- Moralizing
- Neutral

- Objective
- Patriotic
- Persuasive
- Playful
- Sentimental
- Serious
- Supportive
- Sympathetic
- Unsupportive

An author's tone is the author's attitude toward their subject and is usually indicated by word choice. If an author's attitude toward their subject is one of disdain, the author will show the subject in a negative light, using deflating words or words that are negatively charged. If an author's attitude toward their subject is one of praise, the author will use agreeable words and show the subject in a positive light. If an author takes a neutral tone towards their subject, their words will be neutral as well, and they probably will show all sides of their subject, not just the negative or positive side.

Style is another indication of the author's attitude and includes aspects such as sentence structure, type of language, and formatting. Sentence structure is how a sentence is put together. Sometimes, short, choppy sentences will indicate a certain tone given the surrounding context, while longer sentences may serve to create a buffer to avoid being too harsh, or may be used to explain additional information. Style may also include formal or informal language. Using formal language to talk about a subject may indicate a level of respect. Using informal language may be used to create an atmosphere of friendliness or familiarity with a subject. Again, it depends on the surrounding context whether or not language is used in a negative or positive way. Style may also include formatting, such as determining the length of paragraphs or figuring out how to address the reader at the very beginning of the text.

The following is a passage from *The Florentine Painters of the Renaissance* by Bernhard Berenson. Following the passage is a question stem regarding the author's attitude toward their subject:

Let us look now at an even greater triumph of movement than the Nudes, Pollaiuolo's "Hercules Strangling Antæus." As you realise the suction of Hercules' grip on the earth, the swelling of his calves with the pressure that falls on them, the violent throwing back of his chest, the stifling force of his embrace; as you realise the supreme effort of Antæus, with one hand crushing down upon the head and the other tearing at the arm of Hercules, you feel as if a fountain of energy had sprung up under your feet and were playing through your veins. I cannot refrain from mentioning still another masterpiece, this time not only of movement, but of tactile values and personal beauty as well—Pollaiuolo's "David" at Berlin. The young warrior has sped his stone, cut off the giant's head, and now he strides over it, his graceful, slender figure still vibrating with the rapidity of his triumph, expectant, as if fearing the ease of it. What lightness, what buoyancy we feel as we realise the movement of this wonderful youth!

Which one of the following best captures the author's attitude toward the paintings depicted in the passage?
   a. Neutrality towards the subject in this passage.
   b. Disdain for the violence found in the paintings.
   c. Excitement for the physical beauty found within the paintings.
   d. Passion for the movement and energy of the paintings.
   e. Seriousness for the level of artistry the paintings hold.

Choice *D* is the best answer. We know that the author feels positively about the subject because of the word choice. Berenson uses words and phrases like "supreme," "fountain of energy," "graceful," "figure still vibrating," "lightness," "buoyancy," and "wonderful youth." Notice also the exclamation mark at the end of the paragraph. These words and style depict an author full of passion, especially for the movement and energy found within the paintings.

Choice *A* is incorrect because the author is biased towards the subject due to the energy he writes with— he calls the movement in the paintings "wonderful" and by the other word choices and phrases, readers can tell that this is not an objective analysis of these paintings. Choice *B* is incorrect because, although the author does mention the "violence" in the stance of Hercules, he does not exude disdain towards this. Choice *C* is incorrect. There is excitement in the author's tone, and some of this excitement is directed towards the paintings' physical beauty. However, this is not the *best* answer choice. Choice *D* is more accurate when stating the passion is for the movement and energy of the paintings, of which physical beauty is included. Finally, Choice *E* is incorrect. The tone is partly serious, but we see the author getting carried away with enthusiasm for the beauty of the paintings towards the middle and especially the end of the passage.

The Impact of New Information on Claims or Arguments in the Selection

Another useful skill in the LSAT Reading Comprehension section is being able to use new information from the question stem to apply to a claim in the passage. Most of the "new information" questions in the LSAT Reading Comprehension are *strengthening* or *weakening* questions, where the question will ask which of the information in the answer choices best strengthens or weakens a given claim. It's important to read the passage a few times first in order to understand the original claim's stance. Below is a list of questions that might fall under the "new information" question stems:

- Which of the following, if true, best strengthens the author's claim?
- Which of the following, if true, most weakens the author's claim?
- Which of the following, if true, best supports the author's argument that says . . .?
- Which of the following, if true, most undermines the author's claim that says . . .?

The new information question stems will contain a synonym of the word "strengthens" or "weakens," such as "bolsters," "supports," or "undermines," and will also display the statement "if true." The latter is to make sure the test taker does not question the validity of the information in a real-world context. Just like stated above, everything in the passage or in the question stem will be assumed to be true unless otherwise stated or put into question by the stem. The following is an example of a strengthening question:

For elementary-age students, the biggest sports-related injuries are concussions incurred while playing soccer. The popular assumption is that football is more prone to causing concussions, but this is not the case for this age group. I think it would greatly benefit our school if we required our soccer players to wear helmets.

Which of the following, if true, best strengthens the author's claim above?
>   a. Concussions are not life-threatening, so students should not be required to wear helmets during soccer games.
>   b. Major concussions can limit a student's ability to read, write, and focus on schoolwork or any other work that demands mental attention.
>   c. The school board will give a monetary incentive to any school sports program that adopts helmets.
>   d. Forcing soccer players to wear helmets would be humiliating if they were playing a team that wasn't required to wear helmets.
>   e. We should get rid of soccer altogether since it causes elementary-age students the most concussions out of any sport.

Choice *C* is the best answer because it strengthens the author's claim by presenting an even stronger reason for requiring soccer players to wear helmets. If we as readers know that there is another advantage to accepting the author's claim that players should wear helmets besides preventing concussions, then the claim is strengthened.

Choice *A* is incorrect because it states that concussions are not life-threatening. This logic does not help the argument in question, that the school would benefit from requiring students to wear helmets.

Choice *B* is tricky because it builds upon a premise in the argument. However, the author's claim is not convincing us that concussions are dangerous. The author's claim is that the school would greatly benefit from requiring players to wear helmets during soccer. This choice is close, but it is not the best choice.

Choice *D* also goes against the argument in question—the argument is that requiring soccer players to wear helmets would benefit the school, and Choice *D* gives reason *not* to require soccer players to wear helmets. This choice weakens the claim.

Choice *E* goes beyond the argument. This choice doesn't strengthen the claim; it provides another claim altogether. This choice is incorrect.

In the above example of a strengthening question, we see which new information (answer choices) strengthens the claim presented in the passage. Let's take a look at a weakening question:

Last Sunday at the Lincolnville picnic, the town ate every single one of my mom's chocolate brownies. My mom makes the best dessert in Lincolnville.

Which of the following, if true, most undermines the author's claim above?
>   a. My mom went to cooking school and has her own television show dedicated to dessert recipes.
>   b. My mom also brought potato salad to the picnic, but no one ate it.
>   c. There were 250 people at the town picnic.
>   d. My mom won the town award for "tastiest treats."
>   e. Chocolate brownies were the only dessert brought to the picnic.

This is a basic form of a weakening question. The question stem has a premise (the town ate every single one of my mom's chocolate brownies) and a conclusion (my mom makes the best dessert in Lincolnville). In strengthening and weakening questions, it's important to look for a bridge between the premise and conclusion that will either hurt or help the conclusion. Choice *E* is the best answer choice because it most undermines, or weakens, the author's conclusion that the mom makes the best dessert in Lincolnville. If the speaker's only proof that the mom makes the best dessert in Lincolnville is that the town ate all the brownies, then the fact that brownies were the *only* dessert makes us think the town ate the brownies because that was the only option, not because they were the best dessert.

Choices *A* and *D* serve to strengthen the claim, not to weaken it. Choice *B* does not weaken or strengthen the claim, because the claim has to do with desserts, and this answer choice is about potato salad. Choice *C* is incorrect because we don't know how big the town is to make a judgment on whether 250 people is an adequate representation of the community.

Again, most strengthening and weakening questions will provide some sort of gap between its premise and conclusion. The new information will make that gap stronger, weaken the gap, or be irrelevant to the claim altogether. Try not to get lost in the wording of the new information; rather, plug the new information in the passage and see how the new information works—that is, does it strengthen the claim or weaken the claim?

Practice Questions

Questions 1-6 are based on the following passage from The Life, Crime, and Capture of John Wilkes Booth *by George Alfred Townsend:*

The box in which the President sat consisted of two boxes turned into one, the middle partition being removed, as on all occasions when a state party visited the theater. The box was on a level with the dress circle; about twelve feet above the stage. There were two entrances—the door nearest to the wall having been closed and locked; the door nearest the balustrades of the dress circle, and at right angles with it, being open and left open, after the visitors had entered. The interior was carpeted, lined with crimson paper, and furnished with a sofa covered with crimson velvet, three arm chairs similarly covered, and six cane-bottomed chairs. Festoons of flags hung before the front of the box against a background of lace.

President Lincoln took one of the arm-chairs and seated himself in the front of the box, in the angle nearest the audience, where, partially screened from observation, he had the best view of what was transpiring on the stage. Mrs. Lincoln sat next to him, and Miss Harris in the opposite angle nearest the stage. Major Rathbone sat just behind Mrs. Lincoln and Miss Harris. These four were the only persons in the box.

The play proceeded, although "Our American Cousin," without Mr. Sothern, has, since that gentleman's departure from this country, been justly esteemed a very dull affair. The audience at Ford's, including Mrs. Lincoln, seemed to enjoy it very much. The worthy wife of the President leaned forward, her hand upon her husband's knee, watching every scene in the drama with amused attention. Even across the President's face at intervals swept a smile, robbing it of its habitual sadness.

About the beginning of the second act, the mare, standing in the stable in the rear of the theater, was disturbed in the midst of her meal by the entrance of the young man who had quitted her in the afternoon. It is presumed that she was saddled and bridled with exquisite care.

Having completed these preparations, Mr. Booth entered the theater by the stage door; summoned one of the scene shifters, Mr. John Spangler, emerged through the same door with that individual, leaving the door open, and left the mare in his hands to be held until he (Booth) should return. Booth who was even more fashionably and richly dressed than usual, walked thence around to the front of the theater, and went in. Ascending to the dress circle, he stood for a little time gazing around upon the audience and occasionally upon the stage in his usual graceful manner. He was subsequently observed by Mr. Ford, the proprietor of the theater, to be slowly elbowing his way through the crowd that packed the rear of the dress circle toward the right side, at the extremity of which was the box where Mr. and Mrs. Lincoln and their companions were seated. Mr. Ford casually noticed this as a slightly extraordinary symptom of interest on the part of an actor so familiar with the routine of the theater and the play.

1. Which of the following best describes the author's attitude toward the events leading up to the assassination of President Lincoln?
   a. Excitement, due to the setting and its people
   b. Sadness, due to the death of a beloved president
   c. Anger, due to the impending violence
   d. Neutrality, due to the style of the report
   e. Apprehension, due to the crowd and their ignorance

2. What does the author mean by the last sentence in the passage?
   a. Mr. Ford was suspicious of Booth and assumed he was making his way to Mr. Lincoln's box.
   b. Mr. Ford assumed Booth's movement throughout the theater was due to being familiar with the theater.
   c. Mr. Ford thought that Booth was making his way to the theater lounge to find his companions.
   d. Mr. Ford thought that Booth was elbowing his way to the dressing room to get ready for the play.
   e. Mr. Ford thought that Booth was coming down with an illness due to the strange symptoms he displayed.

3. Given the author's description of the play "Our American Cousin," which one of the following is most analogous to Mr. Sothern's departure from the theater?
   a. A ballet dancer who leaves the New York City Ballet just before they go on to their final performance.
   b. A basketball player leaves an NBA team and the next year they make it to the championship but lose.
   c. A lead singer leaves their band to begin a solo career, and the band's sales on their next album drop by 50 percent.
   d. A movie actor who dies in the middle of making a movie and the movie is made anyway by actors who resemble the deceased.
   e. A professor who switches to the top-rated university for their department only to find the university they left behind has surpassed his new department's rating.

4. Which of the following texts most closely relates to the organizational structure of the passage?
   a. A chronological account in a fiction novel of a woman and a man meeting for the first time.
   b. A cause-and-effect text ruminating on the causes of global warming.
   c. An autobiography that begins with the subject's death and culminates in his birth.
   d. A text focusing on finding a solution to the problem of the Higgs boson particle.
   e. A text contrasting the realities of life on Mars versus life on Earth.

5. Which of the following words, if substituted for the word *festoons* in the first paragraph, would LEAST change the meaning of the sentence?
   a. Feathers
   b. Armies
   c. Adornments
   d. Buckets
   e. Boats

6. What is the primary purpose of the passage?
   a. To persuade the audience that John Wilkes Booth killed Abraham Lincoln
   b. To inform the audience of the setting wherein Lincoln was shot
   c. To narrate the bravery of Lincoln and his last days as President
   d. To recount in detail the events that led up to Abraham Lincoln's death
   e. To disprove the popular opinion that John Wilkes Booth is the person who killed Abraham Lincoln

Questions 7-13 are based on the following passage from The Story of Germ Life *by Herbert William Conn:*

The first and most universal change effected in milk is its souring. So universal is this phenomenon that it is generally regarded as an inevitable change that cannot be avoided, and, as already pointed out, has in the past been regarded as a normal property of milk. To-day, however, the phenomenon is well understood. It is due to the action of certain of the milk bacteria upon the milk sugar which converts it into lactic acid, and this acid gives the sour taste and curdles the milk. After this acid is produced in small quantity its presence proves deleterious to the growth of the bacteria, and further bacterial growth is checked. After souring, therefore, the milk for some time does not ordinarily undergo any further changes.

Milk souring has been commonly regarded as a single phenomenon, alike in all cases. When it was first studied by bacteriologists it was thought to be due in all cases to a single species of micro-organism which was discovered to be commonly present and named *Bacillus acidi lactici*. This bacterium has certainly the power of souring milk rapidly, and is found to be very common in dairies in Europe. As soon as bacteriologists turned their attention more closely to the subject it was found that the spontaneous souring of milk was not always caused by the same species of bacterium. Instead of finding this *Bacillus acidi lactici* always present, they found that quite a number of different species of bacteria have the power of souring milk, and are found in different specimens of soured milk. The number of species of bacteria that have been found to sour milk has increased until something over a hundred are known to have this power. These different species do not affect the milk in the same way. All produce some acid, but they differ in the kind and the amount of acid, and especially in the other changes which are effected at the same time that the milk is soured, so that the resulting soured milk is quite variable. In spite of this variety, however, the most recent work tends to show that the majority of cases of spontaneous souring of milk are produced by bacteria which, though somewhat variable, probably constitute a single species, and are identical with the *Bacillus acidi lactici*. This species, found common in the dairies of Europe, according to recent investigations occurs in this country as well. We may say, then, that while there are many species of bacteria infesting the dairy which can sour the milk, there is one that is more common and more universally found than others, and this is the ordinary cause of milk souring.

When we study more carefully the effect upon the milk of the different species of bacteria found in the dairy, we find that there is a great variety of changes they produce when they are allowed to grow in milk. The dairyman experiences many troubles with his milk. It sometimes curdles without becoming acid. Sometimes it becomes bitter, or acquires an unpleasant "tainted" taste, or, again, a "soapy" taste. Occasionally, a dairyman finds his milk becoming slimy, instead of souring and curdling in the normal fashion. At such times, after a number of hours, the milk becomes so slimy that it can be drawn into long threads. Such an infection proves very troublesome, for many a time it persists in spite of all attempts made to remedy it. Again, in other cases the milk will turn blue, acquiring about the time it becomes sour a beautiful sky-blue colour. Or it may become red, or occasionally yellow. All of these troubles the dairyman owes to the presence in his milk of unusual species of bacteria which grow there abundantly.

7. The word *deleterious* in the first paragraph can be best interpreted as meaning which one of the following?
    a. Amicable
    b. Smoldering
    c. Luminous
    d. Ruinous
    e. Virtuous

8. Which of the following best explains how the passage is organized?

a. The author begins by presenting the effects of a phenomenon, then explains the process of this phenomenon, and then ends by giving the history of the study of this phenomenon.

b. The author begins by explaining a process or phenomenon, then gives the history of the study of this phenomenon, this ends by presenting the effects of this phenomenon.

c. The author begins by giving the history of the study of a certain phenomenon, then explains the process of this phenomenon, then ends by presenting the effects of this phenomenon.

d. The author begins by giving a broad definition of a subject, then presents more specific cases of the subject, then ends by contrasting two different viewpoints on the subject.

e. The author begins by contrasting two different viewpoints, then gives a short explanation of a subject, then ends by summarizing what was previously stated in the passage.

9. What is the primary purpose of the passage?

a. To inform the reader of the phenomenon, investigation, and consequences of milk souring

b. To persuade the reader that milk souring is due to *Bacillus acidi lactici,* which is commonly found in the dairies of Europe

c. To describe the accounts and findings of researchers studying the phenomenon of milk souring

d. To discount the former researchers' opinions on milk souring and bring light to new investigations

e. To narrate the story of one researcher who discovered the phenomenon of milk souring and its subsequent effects

10. What does the author say about the ordinary cause of milk souring?

a. Milk souring is caused mostly by a species of bacteria called *Bacillus acidi lactici,* although former research asserted that it was caused by a variety of bacteria.

b. The ordinary cause of milk souring is unknown to current researchers, although former researchers thought it was due to a species of bacteria called *Bacillus acidi lactici.*

c. Milk souring is caused mostly by a species of bacteria identical to that of *Bacillus acidi lactici,* although there are a variety of other bacteria that cause milk souring as well.

d. The ordinary cause of milk souring will sometimes curdle without becoming acidic, though sometimes it will turn colors other than white, or have strange smells or tastes.

e. The ordinary cause of milk souring is from bacteria with a strange, "soapy" smell, usually the color of sky blue.

11. The author of the passage would most likely agree most with which of the following?

a. Milk researchers in the past have been incompetent and have sent us on a wild goose chase when determining what causes milk souring.

b. Dairymen are considered more expert in the field of milk souring than milk researchers.

c. The study of milk souring has improved throughout the years, as we now understand more of what causes milk souring and what happens afterward.

d. Any type of bacteria will turn milk sour, so it's best to keep milk in an airtight container while it is being used.

e. The effects of milk souring is a natural occurrence of milk, so it should not be dangerous to consume.

12. Given the author's account of the consequences of milk souring, which of the following is most closely analogous to the author's description of what happens after milk becomes slimy?
    a. The chemical change that occurs when a firework explodes.
    b. A rainstorm that overwaters a succulent plant.
    c. Mercury inside of a thermometer that leaks out.
    d. A child who swallows flea medication.
    e. A large block of ice that melts into a liquid.

13. What type of paragraph would most likely come after the third?
    a. A paragraph depicting the general effects of bacteria on milk.
    b. A paragraph explaining a broad history of what researchers have found in regard to milk souring.
    c. A paragraph outlining the properties of milk souring and the way in which it occurs.
    d. A paragraph showing the ways bacteria infiltrate milk and ways to avoid this infiltration.
    e. A paragraph naming all the bacteria in alphabetical order with a brief definition of what each does to milk.

Questions 14-20 are based on the following two passages, labeled "Passage A" and "Passage B":

Passage A

(from "Free Speech in War Time" by James Parker Hall, written in 1921, published in Columbia Law Review, Vol. 21 No. 6)

In approaching this problem of interpretation, we may first put out of consideration certain obvious limitations upon the generality of all guaranties of free speech. An occasional unthinking malcontent may urge that the only meaning not fraught with danger to liberty is the literal one that no utterance may be forbidden, no matter what its intent or result; but in fact, it is nowhere seriously argued by anyone whose opinion is entitled to respect that direct and intentional incitations to crime may not be forbidden by the state. If a state may properly forbid murder or robbery or treason, it may also punish those who induce or counsel the commission of such crimes. Any other view makes a mockery of the state's power to declare and punish offences. And what the state may do to prevent the incitement of serious crimes that are universally condemned, it may also do to prevent the incitement of lesser crimes, or of those in regard to the bad tendency of which public opinion is divided. That is, if the state may punish John for burning straw in an alley, it may also constitutionally punish Frank for inciting John to do it, though Frank did so by speech or writing. And if, in 1857, the United States could punish John for helping a fugitive slave to escape, it could also punish Frank for inducing John to do this, even though a large section of public opinion might applaud John and condemn the Fugitive Slave Law.

Passage B

(from "Freedom of Speech in War Time" by Zechariah Chafee, Jr. written in 1919, published in Harvard Law Review Vol. 32 No. 8)

The true boundary line of the First Amendment can be fixed only when Congress and the courts realize that the principle on which speech is classified as lawful or unlawful involves the balancing against each other of two very important social interests, in public safety and in the search for truth. Every reasonable attempt should be made to maintain both interests unimpaired, and the great interest in free speech should be sacrificed only when the interest in public safety is really imperiled, and not, as most men believe, when it is barely conceivable that it may be slightly affected. In war time, therefore, speech should be unrestricted by the censorship or by punishment, unless it is clearly liable to cause direct and dangerous interference with the conduct of the war.

Thus our problem of locating the boundary line of free speech is solved. It is fixed close to the point where words will give rise to unlawful acts. We cannot define the right of free speech with the precision of the Rule against Perpetuities or the Rule in Shelley's Case, because it involves national policies which are much more flexible than private property, but we can establish a workable principle of classification in this method of balancing and this broad test of certain danger. There is a similar balancing in the determination of what is "due process of law." And we can with certitude declare that the First Amendment forbids the punishment of words merely for their injurious tendencies. The history of the Amendment and the political function of free speech corroborate each other and make this conclusion plain.

14. Which one of the following questions is central to both passages?
    a. Why is freedom of speech something to be protected in the first place?
    b. Do people want absolute liberty or do they only want liberty for a certain purpose?
    c. What is the true definition of freedom of speech in a democracy?
    d. How can we find an appropriate boundary of freedom of speech during wartime?
    e. What is the interpretation of the first amendment and its limitations?

15. The authors of the two passages would be most likely to disagree over which of the following?
    a. A man is thrown in jail due to his provocation of violence in Washington D.C. during a riot.
    b. A man is thrown in jail for stealing bread for his starving family, and the judge has mercy for him and lets him go.
    c. A man is thrown in jail for encouraging a riot against the U.S. government for the wartime tactics although no violence ensues.
    d. A man is thrown in jail because he has been caught as a German spy working within the U.S. army.
    e. A man is thrown in jail because he murdered a German-born citizen whom he thought was working for the Central Powers during World War I.

16. The relationship between Passage A and Passage B is most analogous to the relationship between the documents described in which of the following?
    a. A research report that asserts water pollution in major cities in California has increased by thirty percent in the past five years; an article advocating the cessation of chicken farms in California near rivers to avoid pollution.
    b. An article detailing the effects of radiation in Fukushima; a research report describing the deaths and birth defects as a result of the hazardous waste dumped on the Somali Coast.
    c. An article that suggests that labor laws during times of war should be left up to the states; an article that showcases labor laws during the past that have been altered due to the current crisis of war.
    d. A research report arguing that the leading cause of methane emissions in the world is from agriculture practices; an article citing that the leading cause of methane emissions in the world is from the transportation of coal, oil, and natural gas.
    e. A journal article in the Netherlands about the law of euthanasia that cites evidence to support only the act of passive euthanasia as an appropriate way to die; a journal article in the Netherlands about the law of euthanasia that cites evidence to support voluntary euthanasia in any aspect.

17. The author uses the examples in the last lines of Passage A in order to do what?
    a. To demonstrate different types of crimes for the purpose of comparing them to see by which one the principle of freedom of speech would become objectionable.
    b. To demonstrate that anyone who incites a crime, despite the severity or magnitude of the crime, should be held accountable for that crime in some degree.
    c. To prove that the definition of "freedom of speech" is altered depending on what kind of crime is being committed.
    d. To show that some crimes are in the best interest of a nation and should not be punishable if they are proven to prevent harm to others.
    e. To suggest that the crimes mentioned should be reopened in order to punish those who incited the crimes.

18. Which of the following, if true, would most seriously undermine the claim proposed by the author in Passage A that if the state can punish a crime, then it can punish the incitement of that crime?
    a. The idea that human beings are able and likely to change their mind between the utterance and execution of an event that may harm others.
    b. The idea that human beings will always choose what they think is right based on their cultural upbringing.
    c. The idea that the limitation of free speech by the government during wartime will protect the country from any group that causes a threat to that country's freedom.
    d. The idea that those who support freedom of speech probably have intentions of subverting the government.
    e. The idea that if a man encourages a woman to commit a crime and she succeeds, the man is just as guilty as the woman.

19. What is the primary purpose of the second passage?
    a. To analyze the First Amendment in historical situations in order to make an analogy to the current war at hand in the nation.
    b. To demonstrate that the boundaries set during wartime are different from that when the country is at peace, and that we should change our laws accordingly.
    c. To offer the idea that during wartime, the principle of freedom of speech should be limited to that of even minor utterances in relation to a crime.
    d. To call upon the interpretation of freedom of speech to be already evident in the First Amendment and to offer a clear perimeter of the principle during war time.
    e. To assert that any limitation on freedom of speech is a violation of human rights and that the circumstances of war do not change this violation.

20. Which of the following words, if substituted for the word *malecontent* in Passage A, would LEAST change the meaning of the sentence?
    a. Regimen
    b. Cacophony
    c. Anecdote
    d. Residua
    e. Grievance

Questions 21-27 are based on the following passage from Rhetoric and Poetry in the Renaissance: A Study of Rhetorical Terms in English Renaissance Literary Criticism *by DL Clark:*

To the Greeks and Romans, rhetoric meant the theory of oratory. As a pedagogical mechanism, it endeavored to teach students to persuade an audience. The content of rhetoric included all that the ancients had learned to be of value in persuasive public speech. It taught how to work up a case by drawing valid inferences from sound evidence, how to organize this material in the most persuasive order, and how to compose in clear and harmonious sentences. Thus, to the Greeks and Romans, rhetoric was defined by its function of discovering means to persuasion and was taught in the schools as something that every free-born man could and should learn.

In both these respects the ancients felt that poetics, the theory of poetry, was different from rhetoric. As the critical theorists believed that the poets were inspired, they endeavored less to teach men to be poets than to point out the excellences which the poets had attained. Although these critics generally, with the exceptions of Aristotle and Eratosthenes, believed the greatest value of poetry to be in the teaching of morality, no one of them endeavored to define poetry, as they did rhetoric, by its purpose. To Aristotle, and centuries later to Plutarch, the distinguishing mark of poetry was imitation. Not until the renaissance did critics define poetry as an art of imitation endeavoring to inculcate morality . . .

The same essential difference between classical rhetoric and poetics appears in the content of classical poetics. Whereas classical rhetoric deals with speeches which might be delivered to convict or acquit a defendant in the law court, or to secure a certain action by the deliberative assembly, or to adorn an occasion, classical poetic deals with lyric, epic, and drama. It is a commonplace that classical literary critics paid little attention to the lyric. It is less frequently realized that they devoted almost as little space to discussion of metrics. By far the greater bulk of classical treatises on poetics is devoted to characterization and to the technique of plot construction, involving as it does narrative and dramatic unity and movement as distinct from logical unity and movement.

21. What does the author say about one way in which the purpose of poetry changed for later philosophers?
    a. The author says that at first, poetry was not defined by its purpose but was valued for its ability to be used to teach morality. Later, some philosophers would define poetry by its ability to instill morality. Finally, during the renaissance, poetry was believed to be an imitative art, but was not necessarily believed to instill morality in its readers.
    b. The author says that the classical understanding of poetry dealt with its ability to be used to teach morality. Later, philosophers would define poetry by its ability to imitate life. Finally, during the renaissance, poetry was believed to be an imitative art that instilled morality in its readers.
    c. The author says that at first, poetry was thought to be an imitation of reality, then later, philosophers valued poetry more for its ability to instill morality.
    d. The author says that the classical understanding of poetry was that it dealt with the search for truth through its content; later, the purpose of poetry would be through its entertainment value.
    e. The author says that the initial understanding of the purpose of poetry was its entertainment value. Then, as poetry evolved into a more religious era, the renaissance, it was valued for its ability to instill morality through its teaching.

22. What does the author of the passage say about classical literary critics in relation to poetics?
    a. That rhetoric was valued more than poetry because rhetoric had a definitive purpose to persuade an audience, and poetry's wavering purpose made it harder for critics to teach.
    b. That although most poetry was written as lyric, epic, or drama, the critics were most focused on the techniques of lyric and epic and their performance of musicality and structure.
    c. That although most poetry was written as lyric, epic, or drama, the critics were most focused on the techniques of the epic and drama and their performance of structure and character.
    d. That the study of poetics was more pleasurable than the study of rhetoric due to its ability to assuage its audience, and the critics, therefore, focused on what poets did to create that effect.
    e. That since poetics was made by the elite in Greek and Roman society, literary critics resented poetics for its obsession of material things and its superfluous linguistics.

23. What is the primary purpose of this passage?
    a. To alert the readers to Greek and Roman culture regarding poetic texts and the focus on characterization and plot construction rather than lyric and meter.
    b. To inform the readers of the changes in poetic critical theory throughout the years and to contrast those changes to the solidity of rhetoric.
    c. To educate the audience on rhetoric by explaining the historical implications of using rhetoric in the education system.
    d. To convince the audience that poetics is a subset of rhetoric as viewed by the Greek and Roman culture.
    e. To contemplate the differences between classical rhetoric and poetry and to consider their purposes in a particular culture.

24. The word *inculcate* in the second paragraph can be best interpreted as meaning which one of the following?
    a. Imbibe
    b. Instill
    c. Implode
    d. Inquire
    e. Idolize

25. Which of the following most closely resembles the way in which the passage is structured?
    a. The first paragraph presents an issue. The second paragraph offers a solution to the problem. The third paragraph summarizes the first two paragraphs.
    b. The first paragraph presents definitions and examples of a particular subject. The second paragraph presents a second subject in the same way. The third paragraph offers a contrast of the two subjects.
    c. The first paragraph presents an inquiry. The second paragraph explains the details of that inquiry. The last paragraph offers a solution.
    d. The first paragraph presents two subjects alongside definitions and examples. The second paragraph presents us a comparison of the two subjects. The third paragraph presents a contrast of the two subjects.
    e. The first paragraph offers a solution to a problem. The second paragraph questions the solution. The third paragraph offers a different solution.

26. Given the author's description of the content of rhetoric in the first paragraph, which one of the following is most analogous to what it taught? (The sentence is shown below.)

It taught how to work up a case by drawing valid inferences from sound evidence, how to organize this material in the most persuasive order, how to compose in clear and harmonious sentences.

    a. As a musician, they taught me that the end product of the music is everything—what I did to get there was irrelevant, whether it was my ability to read music or the reliance on my intuition to compose.

    b. As a detective, they taught me that time meant everything when dealing with a new case, that the simplest explanation is usually the right one, and that documentation is extremely important to credibility.

    c. As a writer, they taught me the most important thing about writing was consistently showing up to the page every single day, no matter where my muse was.

    d. As a football player, they taught me how to understand the logistics of the game, how my placement on the field affected the rest of the team, and how to run and throw with a mixture of finesse and strength.

    e. As a doctor, they taught me how to show compassion towards patients and how to take care of my own physical and mental health while running my own practice.

27. Which of the following words, if substituted for the word *treatises* in paragraph two, would LEAST change the meaning of the sentence?

    a. Thesauruses

    b. Encyclopedias

    c. Sermons

    d. Anthems

    e. Commentary

Answer Explanations

1. D: Neutrality due to the style of the report. The report is mostly objective; we see very little language that entails any strong emotion whatsoever. The story is told almost as an objective documentation of a sequence of actions—we see the president sitting in his box with his wife, their enjoyment of the show, Booth's walk through the crowd to the box, and Ford's consideration of Booth's movements. There is perhaps a small amount of bias when the author mentions the president's "worthy wife." However, the word choice and style show no signs of excitement, sadness, anger, or apprehension from the author's perspective, so the best answer is Choice *D*.

2. B: Mr. Ford assumed Booth's movement throughout the theater was due to being familiar with the theater. Choice *A* is incorrect; although Booth does eventually make his way to Lincoln's box, Mr. Ford does not make this distinction in this part of the passage. Choice *C* is incorrect; although the passage mentions "companions," it mentions Lincoln's companions rather than Booth's companions. Choice *D* is incorrect; the passage mentions "dress circle," which means the first level of the theater, but this is different from a "dressing room." Finally, Choice *E* is incorrect; the passage mentions a "symptom" but does not signify a symptom from an illness.

3. C: A lead singer leaves their band to begin a solo career, and the band's sales on their next album drop by 50 percent. The original source of the analogy displays someone significant to an event who leaves, and then the event becomes the worst for it. We see Mr. Sothern leaving the theater company, and then the play becoming a "very dull affair." Choice *A* depicts a dancer who backs out of an event before the final performance, so this is incorrect. Choice *B* shows a basketball player leaving an event, and then the team makes it to the championship but then loses. This choice could be a contestant for the right answer; however, we don't know if the team has become the worst for his departure or the better for it. We simply do not have enough information here. Choice *D* is incorrect. The actor departs an event, but there is no assessment of the quality of the movie. It simply states what actors filled in instead. Choice *E* is incorrect because the opposite of the source happens; the professor leaves the entity, and the entity becomes better. Additionally, the betterment of the entity is not due to the individual leaving. Choice *E* is not analogous to the source.

4. A: A chronological account in a fiction novel of a woman and a man meeting for the first time. It's tempting mark Choice *A* wrong because the genres are different. Choice *A* is a fiction text, and the original passage is not a fictional account. However, the question stem asks specifically for organizational structure. Choice *A* is a chronological structure just like the passage, so this is the correct answer. The passage does not have a cause and effect, problem/solution, or compare/contrast structure, making Choices *B*, *D*, and *E* incorrect. Choice *C* is tempting because it mentions an autobiography; however, the structure of this text starts at the end and works its way toward the beginning, which is the opposite structure of the original passage.

5. C: The word *adornments* would LEAST change the meaning of the sentence because it's the most closely related word to *festoons*. The other choices don't make sense in the context of the sentence. *Feathers* of flags, *armies* of flags, *buckets* of flags, and *boats* of flags are not as accurate as the word *adornments* of flags. The passage also talks about other décor in the setting, so the word *adornments* fits right in with the context of the paragraph.

6. D: The primary purpose of the passage is to recount in detail the events that led up to Abraham Lincoln's death. Choice *A* is incorrect; the author makes no claims and uses no rhetoric of persuasion towards the audience. Choice *B* is incorrect, though it's a tempting choice; the passage depicts the setting in exorbitant detail, but the setting itself is not the primary purpose of the passage. Choice *C* is incorrect; one could argue this is a narrative, and the passage is about Lincoln's last few hours, but this isn't the *best* choice. The best choice recounts the details that leads up to Lincoln's death. Finally, Choice *E* is incorrect. The author does not try to prove or disprove anything to the audience, and the passage does not even make it to when Lincoln gets shot, so this part of the story is irrelevant.

7. D: The word *deleterious* can be best interpreted as referring to the word *ruinous*. The first paragraph attempts to explain the process of milk souring, so the "acid" would probably prove "ruinous" to the growth of bacteria and cause souring. Choice *A, amicable*, means friendly, so this does not make sense in context. Choice *B, smoldering*, means to boil or simmer, so this is also incorrect. Choices *C* and *E*, *luminous* and *virtuous*, have positive connotations and don't make sense in the context of the passage. Luminous means shining or brilliant, and virtuous means to be honest or ethical.

8. B: The author begins by explaining a process or phenomenon, then gives the history of the study of this phenomenon, and ends by presenting the effects of this phenomenon. The author explains the process of souring in the first paragraph by informing the reader that "it is due to the action of certain of the milk bacteria upon the milk sugar which converts it into lactic acid, and this acid gives the sour taste and curdles the milk." In the second paragraph, we see how the phenomenon of milk souring was viewed when it was "first studied," and then we proceed to gain insight into "recent investigations" toward the end of the paragraph. Finally, the passage ends by presenting the effects of the phenomenon of milk souring. We see the milk curdling, becoming bitter, tasting soapy, turning blue, or becoming thread-like. All of the other answer choices are incorrect.

9: A: The primary purpose is to inform the reader of the phenomenon, investigation, and consequences of milk souring. Choice *B* is incorrect because the passage states that *Bacillus acidi lactici* is not the only cause of milk souring. Choice *C* is incorrect because, although the author mentions the findings of researchers, the main purpose of the text does not seek to describe their accounts and findings, as we are not even told the names of any of the researchers. Choice *D* is tricky. We do see the author present us with new findings in contrast to the first cases studied by researchers. However, this information is only in the second paragraph, so it is not the primary purpose of the *entire passage*. Finally, Choice *E* is incorrect because the genre of the passage is more informative than narrative, although the author does talk about the phenomenon of milk souring and its subsequent effects.

10. C: Milk souring is caused mostly by a species of bacteria identical to that of *Bacillus acidi lactici* although there are a variety of other bacteria that cause milk souring as well. Choice *A* is incorrect because it contradicts the assertion that the souring is still caused by a variety of bacteria. Choice *B* is incorrect because the ordinary cause of milk souring *is known* to current researchers. Choice *D* is incorrect because this names mostly the effects of milk souring, not the cause. Choice *E* is incorrect because the bacteria itself doesn't have a strange soapy smell or is a different color, but it eventually will cause the milk to produce these effects.

11. C: The study of milk souring has improved throughout the years, as we now understand more of what causes milk souring and what happens afterward. None of the choices here are explicitly stated, so we have to rely on our ability to make inferences. Choice *A* is incorrect because there is no indication from the author that milk researchers in the past have been incompetent—only that recent research has done a better job of studying the phenomenon of milk souring. Choice *B* is incorrect because the author refers to dairymen in relation to the effects of milk souring and their "troubles" surrounding milk souring, and does not compare them to milk researchers. Choice *D* is incorrect because we are told in the second paragraph that only certain types of bacteria are able to sour milk. Choice *E* is incorrect; although we are told that milk souring is a natural occurrence, the author makes no implication that soured milk is safe to consume. Choice *C* is the best answer choice here because although the author does not directly state that the study of milk souring has improved, we can see this might be true due to the comparison of old studies to newer studies, and the fact that the newer studies are being used as a reference in the passage.

12. A: It is most analogous to the chemical change that occurs when a firework explodes. The author tells us that after milk becomes slimy, "it persists in spite of all attempts made to remedy it," which means the milk has gone through a chemical change. It has changed its state from milk to sour milk by changing its odor, color, and material. After a firework explodes, there is nothing one can do to change the substance of a firework back to its original form—the original substance is turned into sound and light. Choice *B* is incorrect because, although the rain overwatered the plant, it's possible that the plant is able to recover from this. Choice *C* is incorrect because although mercury leaking out may be dangerous, the actual substance itself stays the same and does not alter into something else. Choice *D* is incorrect; this situation is not analogous to the alteration of a substance. Choice *E* is also incorrect. Ice melting into a liquid is a physical change, which means it can be undone. Milk turning sour, as the author asserts, cannot be undone.

13. D: It would most likely be a paragraph showing the ways bacteria infiltrate milk and ways to avoid this infiltration. Choices *A, B,* and *C* are incorrect because these are already represented in the third, second, and first paragraphs. Choice *E* is incorrect; this choice isn't impossible. There could be a glossary right after the third paragraph, but this would be an awkward place for a glossary. Choice *D* is the best answer because it follows a sort of problem/solution structure in writing.

14. E: A central question to both passages is: What is the interpretation of the first amendment and its limitations? Choice *A* is incorrect; this is a question for the first passage but it does not apply to the second. Choice *B* is incorrect; a quote mentions this at the end of the first passage, but this question is not found in the second passage. Choice *C* is incorrect, as the passages are not concerned with the definition of freedom of speech, but how to interpret it. Choice *D* is incorrect; this is a question for the second passage, but it is not found in the first passage.

15. C: The authors would most likely disagree over the man thrown in jail for encouraging a riot against the U.S. government for the wartime tactics although no violence ensued. The author of Passage A says that "If a state may properly forbid murder or robbery or treason, it may also punish those who induce or counsel the commission of such crimes." This statement tells us that the author of Passage A would support throwing the man in jail for encouraging a riot, although no violence ensues. The author of Passage B states that "And we can with certitude declare that the First Amendment forbids the punishment of words merely for their injurious tendencies." This is the best answer choice because we are clear on each author's stance in this situation. Choice *A* is tricky; the author of Passage A would definitely agree with this, but it's questionable whether the author of Passage B would also agree. Violence does ensue at the capitol as a result of this man's provocation, and the author of Passage B states "speech should be unrestricted by censorship . . . unless it is clearly liable to cause direct . . . interference with the conduct of war." This answer is close, but it is not the *best* choice. Choice *B* is incorrect because we have no way of knowing what the authors' philosophies are in this situation. Choice *D* is incorrect because, again, we have no way of knowing what the authors would do in this situation, although it's assumed they would probably both agree with this. Choice *E* is something the authors would probably both agree on, because brutal violence ensued, but it has nothing to do with free speech, so we have no way of knowing for sure.

16. E: Choice *E* is the best answer. To figure out the correct answer choice we must find out the relationship between Passage A and Passage B. Between the two passages, we have a general principle (freedom of speech) that is questioned on the basis of interpretation. In Choice *E*, we see that we have a general principle (right to die, or euthanasia) that is questioned on the basis of interpretation as well. Should euthanasia only include passive euthanasia, or euthanasia in any aspect? Choice *A* is a problem/solution relationship; the first option outlines a problem, and the second option delivers a solution, so this choice is incorrect. Choice *B* is incorrect because it does not question the interpretation of a principle, but rather describes the effects of two events that happened in the past involving contamination of radioactive substances. Choice *C* begins with a principle—that of labor laws during wartime—but in the second option, the interpretation isn't questioned. The second option looks at the historical precedent of labor laws in the past during wartime. Choice *D* is incorrect because the two texts disagree over the cause of something rather than the interpretation of it.

17. B: Choice *B* is the best answer choice because the author is trying to demonstrate via the examples that anyone who incites a crime, despite the severity or magnitude of the crime, should be held accountable for that crime in some degree. Choice *A* is incorrect because the crimes mentioned are not being compared to each other, but they are being used to demonstrate a point. Choice *C* is incorrect because the author makes the same point using both of the examples and does not question the definition of freedom of speech but its ability to be limited. Choice *D* is incorrect because this sentiment goes against what the author has been arguing throughout the passage. Choice *E* is incorrect because the author does not suggest that the crimes mentioned be reopened anywhere in the passage.

18. A: The idea that human beings are able and likely to change their mind between the utterance and execution of an event that may harm others most seriously undermines the claim because it brings into question the bad tendency of a crime and points out the difference between utterance and action in moral situations. Choice *B* is incorrect; this idea does not undermine the claim at hand, but introduces an observation irrelevant to the claim. Choices *C, D,* and *E* would most likely strengthen the argument's claim; or, they are at least supported by the author in Passage A.

19. D: The primary purpose is to call upon the interpretation of freedom of speech to be already evident in the First Amendment and to offer a clear perimeter of the principle during war time. Choice *A* is incorrect; the passage calls upon no historical situations as precedent in this passage. Choice *B* is incorrect; we can infer that the author would not agree with this, because the author states that "In war time, therefore, speech should be unrestricted . . . by punishment." Choice *C* is incorrect; this is more consistent with the main idea of the first passage. Choice *E* is incorrect; the passage states a limitation in saying that "speech should be unrestricted . . . unless it is clearly liable to cause direct and dangerous interference with the conduct of war."

20. E: The word that would least change the meaning of the sentence is *grievance. Malcontent* is a complaint or grievance, and in this context would be uttered in advocation of absolute freedom of speech. Choice *A, regimen,* means a pattern of living, and would not make sense in this context. Choice *B, cacophony,* means a harsh noise or mix of discordant noises; someone may express or "urge" a cacophony but it would be an awkward word in this context. Choice *C, anecdote,* is a short account of an amusing story. Since the word is a noun, it fits grammatically inside the sentence, but anecdotes are usually thought out, and this word is considered "unthinking." Choice *D, residua,* means an outcome, and also does not make sense within this context.

21. B: The author says that the classical understanding of poetry dealt with its ability to be used to teach morality. Later, philosophers would define poetry by its ability to imitate life. Finally, during the renaissance, poetry was believed to be an imitative art that instilled morality in its readers. The rest of the answer choices improperly interpret this explanation in the passage. Poetry was never mentioned for use in entertainment, which makes Choices *D* and *E* incorrect. Choices *A* and *C* are incorrect because they mix up the chronological order.

22. C: The author says that although most poetry was written as lyric, epic, or drama, the critics were most focused on the techniques of the epic and drama and their performance of structure and character. This is the best answer choice as portrayed by paragraph three. Choice *A* is incorrect because nowhere in the passage does it say rhetoric was more valued than poetry, although it did seem to have a more definitive purpose than poetry. Choice *B* is incorrect; this almost mirrors Choice *A*, but the critics were *not* focused on the lyric, as the passage indicates. Choice *D* is incorrect because the passage does not mention that the study of poetics was more pleasurable than the study of rhetoric. Choice *E* is incorrect because again, we do not see anywhere in the passage where poetry was reserved for the most elite in society.

23. E: The purpose is to contemplate the differences between classical rhetoric and poetry and to consider their purposes in a particular culture. Choice *A* is incorrect; this thought is discussed in the third paragraph, but it is not the main idea of the passage. Choice *B* is incorrect; although changes in poetics throughout the years is mentioned, this is not the main idea of the passage. Choice *C* is incorrect; although this is partly true—that rhetoric within the education system is mentioned—the subject of poetics is left out of this answer choice. Choice *D* is incorrect; the passage makes no mention of poetics being a subset of rhetoric.

24. B: The correct answer choice is Choice *B*, *instill*. Choice *A*, *imbibe*, means to drink heavily, so this choice is incorrect. Choice *C*, *implode*, means to collapse inward, which does not make sense in this context. Choice *D*, *inquire*, means to investigate. This option is better than the other options, but it is not as accurate as *instill*. Choice *E*, *idolize*, means to admire, which does not make sense in this context.

25. B: The first paragraph presents definitions and examples of a particular subject. The second paragraph presents a second subject in the same way. The third paragraph offers a contrast of the two subjects. In the passage, we see the first paragraph defining rhetoric and offering examples of how the Greeks and Romans taught this subject. In the second paragraph, poetics is defined and examples of its dynamic definition are provided. In the third paragraph, the contrast between rhetoric and poetry is characterized through how each of these were studied in a classical context.

26. D: The best answer is Choice *D:* As a football player, they taught me how to understand the logistics of the game, how my placement on the field affected the rest of the team, and how to run and throw with a mixture of finesse and strength. The content of rhetoric in the passage . . . "taught how to work up a case by drawing valid inferences from sound evidence, how to organize this material in the most persuasive order, and how to compose in clear and harmonious sentences. What we have here is three general principles: 1) it taught me how to understand logic and reason (drawing inferences parallels to understanding the logistics of the game), 2) it taught me how to understand structure and organization (organization of material parallels to organization on the field) and 3) it taught me how to make the end product beautiful (how to compose in harmonious sentences parallels to how to run with finesse and strength). Each part parallels by logic, organization, and style.

27. E: *Treatises* is most closely related to the word *commentary*. Choices *A* and *B* do not make sense because thesauruses and encyclopedias are not written about one single subject. Choice *C* is incorrect; sermons are usually given by religious leaders as advice or teachings. Choice *D* is incorrect; anthems are songs and do not fit within the context of this sentence.

Greetings!

First, we would like to give a huge "thank you" for choosing us and this study guide for your ASWB Bachelors exam. We hope that it will lead you to success on this exam and for your years to come.

Our team has tried to make your preparations as thorough as possible by covering all of the topics you should be expected to know. In addition, our writers attempted to create practice questions identical to what you will see on the day of your actual test. We have also included many test-taking strategies to help you learn the material, maintain the knowledge, and take the test with confidence.

We strive for excellence in our products, and if you have any comments or concerns over the quality of something in this study guide, please send us an email so that we may improve.

As you continue forward in life, we would like to remain alongside you with other books and study guides in our library. We are continually producing and updating study guides in several different subjects. If you are looking for something in particular, all of our products are available on Amazon. You may also send us an email!

Sincerely,
APEX Test Prep
info@apexprep.com

FREE

Free Study Tips DVD

In addition to the tips and content in this guide, we have created a FREE DVD with helpful study tips to further assist your exam preparation. **This FREE Study Tips DVD provides you with top-notch tips to conquer your exam and reach your goals.**

Our simple request in exchange for the strategy-packed DVD packed is that you email us your feedback about our study guide. We would love to hear what you thought about the guide, and we welcome any and all feedback—positive, negative, or neutral. It is our #1 goal to provide you with top-quality products and customer service.

To receive your **FREE Study Tips DVD**, email freedvd@apexprep.com. Please put "FREE DVD" in the subject line and put the following in the email:

   a. The name of the study guide you purchased.

   b. Your rating of the study guide on a scale of 1-5, with 5 being the highest score.

   c. Any thoughts or feedback about your study guide.

   d. Your first and last name and your mailing address, so we know where to send your free DVD!

Thank you!